THE STREET-SMART SALESMAN

HOW GROWING UP POOR HELPED MAKE ME RICH

Anthony Belli
with
Janine Dreyer

WILEY

John Wiley & Sons, Inc.

For Emma, Carmine, Camille, Vinny, and Marian

ISBN 978-1-118-31319-0 (cloth); ISBN 978-1-118-38901-0 (ebk);
ISBN 978-1-118-38899-0 (ebk); ISBN 978-1-118-38898-3 (ebk)

Printed in the United States of America.

10 9 8 7 6 5 4 3 2 1

Contents

Foreword

When Anthony Belli first approached me to write this foreword, I was a bit perplexed. I wondered if and how this author could successfully translate his life experiences into being both the foundation and the basis for his very successful career in sales and sales management. Further, I asked myself if he could effectively correlate those life experiences into successful sales techniques: ones that, if memorialized and employed by other sales executives, could be a tool kit to help them achieve their own success. Having myself grown up in an ethnic, blue-collar Boston community in a family of modest means, Anthony's work and the legitimacy of a "Street-Smart" way of doing things intrigued me.

It is important to note that as a former CEO, I have always admired and respected my salesforce. While many team members contributed, I believe my sales teams were the root cause of my success. They were in the trenches; they were on the front lines. They were facing customers on a daily basis; they were the first line representation of the company to its customer base. Anthony was one of those team members, and his contributions were legendary.

While I enjoyed giving the sales team the opportunity to grow and develop professionally and financially, I retained what I think is a fair trade-off: more equity. As with many professional sales teams, mine were personable, fun loving, and attractive high performers, capable of hard work and outstanding results. Anthony Belli was a very successful and very well compensated member/leader of that and other great sales teams. As you will see, he attributes a great deal of his success to his upbringing, his environment, and the skills, including survival skills, that evolved from that environment.

It is important for the reader to note that the salesforce, as a unit, can and usually does provide the foundation upon which a successful company can be built and its shareholder value enhanced. Despite the often used phrase (and I have heard it from members of several boards of directors) "a great product sells itself," it is an entirely incorrect assumption. Even the best, most innovative products do not sell themselves. I base this statement on countless experiences attempting to introduce innovative new products, whose benefits would seemingly be obvious to any casual observer and especially to a potential customer. One more time: None of these products sold themselves. While great products may make the sales process easier, all products require the competent and relentless execution of a sales plan borne of a sound sales strategy that is in alignment with the company's own corporate goals and strategy. And, in order to execute against these plans, there is need for a professional sales team.

Going beyond that top-down approach, the up-to-date "hunter/killer" sales professional or the street-smart salesperson sets and executes what he or she believes is the most productive individual strategy for penetrating and growing the company's business within the respective sales territory. Anthony argues that the traditional approaches to effective selling are, in many ways, counter to those he advocates and teaches. He says the traditional approaches to selling stressing features, benefits, and price can be least effective in not only setting yourself apart from your peers, but also least effective in getting a customer to agree to do business with you and your company. Anthony's approach, honed on the mean streets of East Harlem in the 1960s, involves the successful use of the very traits that allowed him not only to survive what was a high-risk childhood, but to grow and mature into a highly successful, beautifully attired, and extremely effective sales professional. The lessons Anthony learned growing up were instrumental in his building a successful career in business that has now spanned more than 30 years. The lessons he teaches can, in many instances, be applied to any profession, whether in sales or not.

In preparing this Foreword, I asked the question, "Why is this work important?" Well, based on my own experience leading a number of successful enterprises, successfully employing a motivated and professional sales-force is the very basis for top line growth and ultimately for company success. It is well documented that share-holder value is driven more by revenue growth than by profit growth. And yet, given the extraordinary impact and power over the enterprise's success that a success-ful sales organization can have, many employers do not treat their sales team with the respect and recognition that they deserve. Witness a large healthcare company, where a salesperson pays her dues with two years in the field, often followed by a staff assignment and career path outside of sales. Or better yet, witness a successful sales-person having her territory cut as her production-based compensation was higher than senior executives at the company. Further, few of our best and brightest manage-ment school graduates are encouraged to seek out and aspire to positions in sales and sales management. Very little or no attention is paid to the sales profession or sales as a key topic worthy of study at the nation's top-tier business schools. In fact, if one were to peruse their course offerings, I would bet the number of classes offered with a focus on sales by each of the respective schools to be one or two at most.

And so, you begin this journey by joining Anthony as he traces his childhood and his experiences from the foot-steps of Holy Rosary Elementary School in East Harlem to a career of sales excellence and a very comfortable life. While on this long journey, Anthony observes and picks up tidbits of learning that, in the aggregate, form what he has identified as the street-smart salesperson, one who perseveres, listens, and learns from his customers. And one who creates in the customer's mind a perceived value beyond product features, benefits, and price, while building a sustainable relationship that few other salespeople successfully accomplish. With Anthony, there were and are no excuses common to many salespeople—to wit, the product needs certain features to sell it, the company did not give me the support I needed, and other excuses—a culture lacking accountability. Remembering my own background on the not-so-gentle streets of Boston, I found many of his "street-smart" teachings may be categorized or identified in another way—as good old common sense and as an unparalleled sense of accountability.

Joe Mandato, D.M.
Fellow, The Advanced Leadership Initiative,
Harvard University

Introduction

Dirt Poor to Worry-No-More: Here from There

When I go into Manhattan on business, I often drive the long way home through East Harlem in New York City. That's the neighborhood where I grew up dirt-poor. And, without knowing it, it's where I learned everything I needed to know to become a wealthy, high-performance salesman.

Nowadays I live in Bedford Hills, New York, which is about 40 miles north and about 40 worlds away from East Harlem. But it's still important for me to touch base with my rough and tumble beginnings from time to time, just to acknowledge the source of the street-smarts that have served me so well, the crowded streets and tenements of Italian East Harlem in the 1950s and 1960s. Born into crushing poverty—believe me, it's no overstatement— I got out of Harlem to become a high-performance salesman and a millionaire several times over. And I believe that growing up poor helped make me rich.

Back in July 2007, Janine Dreyer and I walked around the few square blocks that contained my youth. Until that day, I hadn't realized that I hadn't once gotten out of the car in all my many detours through the old neighborhood. I must have been feeling pretty nervous about walking those streets again. Get this: When I changed out of my jogging clothes at the gym that morning, I found that I'd brought two left shoes to wear with my suit and tie.

So there I was, back at Holy Rosary Elementary, this time in sneakers and a Brioni suit, feeling nervous and self-conscious all over again. Because I had lived the first part of my life without a change of clothes or shoes, the Brioni suit trumpeted that things were different for me now, not that anyone in the school office remembered me, of course. Mostly what I remember about Holy Rosary is dull green walls, gentle plaster saints, and hard-ass nuns. I was dumbstruck as soon as we opened the door. The stairwells, hallways, and classrooms were freshly painted in bright colors; there was a music room, an art studio. We toured the hallways and classrooms with a recent graduate just enrolled at Fordham Prep with plans to become a doctor. The gals in the office were glad to do a little search of the file cabinets for my school records—that is, the stack of failing report cards with my name on it—but they came up empty. Everyone agreed my file was probably in one of the old boxes in the basement. Where it belongs!

A year or so before, on another one of my many drive-throughs, I'd seen a Corcoran Real Estate sign on a building at the corner of East 119th Street and Pleasant Avenue, my old stomping grounds. According to their company literature, Corcoran is the largest residential real estate firm in New York City, one of the most expensive cities in the world. I called Corcoran and found out the property was listed for $1.7 million! The more closely I looked, the more I noticed tenement buildings being converted to upscale townhouses, community gardens thriving in open lots left behind some 30 years ago by arson fires.

We headed for my building, 416 East 119th Street. Gone! Nowadays, three buildings—414, 416, and 418—have been combined into two. The entrance to my building, site of many a bull session and hotly contested game of stoopball, was the one that got covered over. The three merged backyards are paved over and, to me, unimaginably free of rubble and garbage. There was even a rookie tree making its way up out of the cement. There was a construction site across the street. A storefront church had replaced Patty Bones's mobbed-up candy store down the block, which had had a pool table in back for the wiseguys.

Along the East River Drive, I saw that the six-acre site of the old Washburn had been leveled. The Washburn Wire Factory—they made extruded wire—took up three city blocks and was one of the biggest industrial employers in Manhattan.[1] In my day, it seemed that every kid I knew had a father, grandfather, brother, and uncle who worked there. The factory limped to a halt in the late 1970s or early 1980s, like pretty much the rest of the city's manufacturing base. Later, reduced to a wreck by negligence, it was sold at a federal auction, the site slated to be demolished to make room for a cluster of big-box stores—Target occupies the site today. I don't know all the implications and complications of gentrification, good or bad, but I do know that change is necessary to survive—and to thrive.

My East Harlem history, tough as it was, is with me every day. And to my lasting benefit.

■ ■ ■

In the 1950s, East Harlem was the country's largest Italian ghetto.[2] It's a little hard to imagine now, post-*Godfather*, what America once thought of its immigrant Italian population. Americans were revolted by the swarthy Italians, who were thought to be lazy, dirty, ignorant, violent, murderous, and traitorous. In the first decades of the twentieth century, many Americans believed that the solution to the nation's rising crime rates was to ban all southern Italians from our shores.[3] Believe me, it was not very long ago that Italians in New York were likely to be not only poor, but despised.

Of the thousands of struggling families in Italian East Harlem, the Bellis (pronounced *bellies*) were among the very poorest. We had nothing when I was a kid, no things, *nothing*. Like countless other poor kids, I spent endless hours fantasizing about how life would be when I was rich and famous, in my case as the star centerfielder for the New York Yankees. I didn't believe I had any useful skills beyond what I could do with a baseball and a bat—and I had the grades to prove it.

Specifically, I would fantasize about the sunny afternoon when I would sign my major league contract and have my picture taken with the owner, manager, and, ideally, Mickey Mantle. It would be hard to overstate the awe I would inspire among the lowlifes in the vicinity of my tenement building if I could only return as a pro ballplayer for a little walk-around. I loved to imagine that, too.

The first thing I was going to do with my money was turn 416 East 119th Street, Apartment 4 (changed, with duct tape, to a 7 in honor of "The Mick"), into a palace—wallpaper, drapery, everything. After that, a fresh coat of paint for every apartment! Call the plumber, Mrs. Aliberti! Call the electrician, the tile man, get the exterminator—it's all on me! I entertained visions of myself donating hundreds and thousands of dollars to good causes, offering wise counsel to countless appreciative people. What I wanted, I came to realize, was to be the transforming hero I craved in my own drama. In writing this book, I'm keeping a promise I made to myself long ago: to share my wealth and knowledge—if I ever got any!

Even though my prospects back then were pretty dim, one thing I couldn't help noticing is that helping someone out makes the giver feel best—while the getter just feels better. As a needy kid, I knew that whenever anybody did anything for me, it felt really, really good to be on the receiving end of some assistance, to have relief from the weight of some burden. Whether that help was offered out of kindness or calculated self-interest made no difference to me. None whatsoever. My memory of that feeling, of how good it feels to be the beneficiary of some real help, is really my secret sales weapon, the basis of the value equation I offer my clients and will show you how to offer yours.

But first, after I gussied up the family tenement, I imagined I'd rebuild Jefferson Park on 114th Street. In my day we didn't refer to Jefferson as a park. We called it the "rock garden." The thin, gray dirt was embedded with stones and metal bottle caps, dusted with cigarette butts and wrappers, sprinkled here and there with broken glass. It was good-for-nothing dirt. I lost two teeth and gained a couple of scars on that dirt, making what would have been routine plays on a carpet of grass. But I always played hard because I was sure that being a Yankee was my only way out of East Harlem. And, boy, did I want out.

Winters, my brother Vinny and I worked our throwing arms in the narrow hallway of the so-called "railroad" apartment and swung our bats in the kitchen. I ate, drank, slept, dreamt, practiced, and studied baseball and nothing else. The game shaped my entire belief system, and throughout my childhood, my obvious talent for it was the one and only thing that gave me any hope for the future.

But this isn't a book about baseball and me. This is a book about the useful skills I picked up on the street and in the alleys, at the schools and in the candy stores of my square-block world, and how those lessons helped me excel at selling and made me a rich man. It was on those mean east side streets that I fine-tuned what I call my "ghetto radar," the ability to spot trouble, remain watchful in a tense situation, identify who might be an ally and who's going to be trouble, and more, on and on, new situations all the time. "Ghetto radar" may not be a very politically correct term, but, truthfully, that's what I call it, so I might as well. I sure don't mean anything derogatory about it. To the contrary.

In Italian East Harlem, what set a person apart and made a lasting impression was an air of confidence, a relaxed manner, and a refusal to be intimidated. The streets and all the apartments were crowded, sometimes very overcrowded. Everywhere I looked, people were struggling for a share: the kids in Catholic school uniforms threading their way through a mix of factory workers, day laborers, black-clad grandmothers, boozehounds, junkies, truants, cops, and wiseguys, people parked on stoops and leaning out the tenement windows. Hookers worked some neighborhood streets; we had a sweet gal, a runaway from Holyoke, Massachusetts, sleep in our apartment from time to time. I learned early to avoid hanging with losers, noticing that junkies hung with junkies, gamblers with gamblers, wiseguys with wiseguys, athletes with athletes (my crowd). Successful business people also must seek their own kind.

Nevertheless, we all have to live in this world together, good and bad, so let's take a moment to discuss the power of positive associations. In general, I found, people want you to share in the things that are central to their world; it's a way of seeking approval. That's why junkies wanted me to do junk with them and wiseguys got some thrills by testing my moral compass. I preferred hanging out with athletes, who just wanted to play ball all day; I loved the competition. But in order to avoid being harassed by the people I didn't want to hang out with, I had to show them some respect—a nod, a wave, a grin—just enough to hold them at bay. To have freedom of movement, you can't alienate people you see every day, no matter what you think of them. If you treat people you disapprove of as invisible, eventually your disregard will move them to anger and they will find ways, big and/or small, to hurt you. You don't want to be on their radar; you want to be able to go about your business unimpeded. So when I say that successful people must seek their own kind, I also caution against expressions of disdain for any-one else. Treat everyone with respect—but choose your own people carefully and keep them close.

Then as now, the struggle of the poor—to stay alive, keep hunger at bay and a roof overhead—is daily and, way too often, lifelong. The struggles of the poor demand not only courage but also stamina, because poverty requires a constant reordering of priorities (food or shoes? heat or electricity?), and every change in priority renews the need for winning strategies and tactics. Such are the flexibilities that I found translated well to sales, which is really an ongoing search for opportunities to be seized. The main difference is that the poor are fighting for a crumb, a tiny piece of someone else's pie, while people in business for themselves are working to sell a sky's-the-limit number of pies baked according to their own recipe.

In this book, I'm going to try to impart my hard-won Street-Smart strategies to all readers regardless of background or present circumstances. If you come from a stable, middle-class background, you will likely have to dig deep even to consider some of the concepts I raise. That's fine. Challenge me; I expect you too. But believe me, I have had many sales reps in my charge cross over to my way of doing things, and we are all the richer for it. *The Street-Smart Salesman* primarily addresses professional salespeople, from entry-level cold callers to wily veterans looking to revamp their game. But smart, curious, and ambitious people in other lines of work who grew up "better" than I did can learn some useful things about humankind in these pages.

First, let me establish my street cred. And let's be clear about one thing up front: I've never done any jail time! My moral compass was forged in the heat of the everyday necessity to "eat without stealing." That's what we called it in our apartment.

Eating Without Stealing: Useful Survival Strategies
East Harlem, NY
1953–1971

1

Birth of a Salesman

Courage is going from failure to failure without losing enthusiasm.

—Winston Churchill (attributed)

I was born in East Harlem in 1953. Until about 1960, Italian East Harlem was one of the Naked City's worst ghettos and the Belli (pronounced "belly") family one of the poorest families in it. Following the race riots of 1964, the lawlessness, looting, and arson fires that decimated poor neighborhoods in cities all across the country came to East Harlem, too. Every other tenement house in our neighborhood was a burned-out ruin, and if you were fortunate enough to live in a tenement that wasn't even smoke-damaged, you can bet the building was in some other advanced state of disrepair. We lived—my mother, father, older brother, sister, and I—in a rundown apartment on East 119th Street. The small, airless rooms strung along a narrow hall like boxcars in a rail yard, baking in summer, freezing in winter.

Generations of lead paint peeled from the cracked plaster. The kitchen/bathroom was at the front of the apartment. The so-called Venetian blinds were broken before I was born and hung at all angles. The frosted glass on the bathroom door had also fallen out before I was born; one panel was covered with scrap plywood, the other with a sheet of banged-up metal. There was no seat on the toilet, no working tub or shower. I took what we colorfully called a "whore's bath" until I was 18 years old, using a sponge or washrag at the kitchen sink, head under the faucet.

Smokers stubbed out their cigarettes on our cracked linoleum floor. Bedsheets were never changed or even washed. Rats, mice, roaches came and went at will. Actually, mice were considered a blessing because if you had mice, the rats went on vacation. Arguably, the rats' living standards exceeded our own.

I can hear you asking: Where were my parents in all this mess? Well, my father was a "molder" in a factory somewhere downtown, one of his two jobs. Even now, I'm not exactly sure what a molder does. We didn't see Dad much, though he had a thousand eyes on Vinny and me, courtesy of his friends and family in the neighborhood. Dad had a girlfriend around the corner; my parents' relationship was very complicated. In 1955, my mother, Emma Anita Lemorrocco, developed multiple sclerosis, just 12 years into their marriage and two years after I was born. Up until she got sick, she and my father had lived in the north Bronx for 10 years, and even had a convertible car. But after her disease set in, my parents fell into poverty and had to go back to East Harlem. Mom's disease was only going to get worse, and then she would die—as she did a full 18 years later. There were no medical treatments for multiple sclerosis and no such thing as full-time home care or Meals on Wheels. No costs were cushioned by the taxpayer; the family took the full hit. It was a hard way to learn the art of living with chaos and few resources, the value of sacrifice, but this knowledge has served me well in my profession.

For nearly two decades, the chaos in my family was complete: hour-to-hour, day-to-day, year in, year out. For the last five years of my mother's life, she was a helpless quadriplegic and received the Catholic Last Rites every few months. Every time I have the flu and find myself confined to bed for a few days, I can't help but imagine what it must have been like for her to be immobilized in pain for all those years in an infested tenement in the highest crime area in New York City with three kids to raise.

Because Mom was sick at a time when there weren't any social programs to help her, the awesome weight of her care fell directly on the family, mostly on my big sister, Camille, and the occasional generosity of others.

My father worked a second job, in the evening, delivering prescriptions for a local drugstore that's still in business. Dad didn't come home until after 11 P.M., but he slept in our apartment every night (he and I shared the "big bed") and he always paid the $42 monthly rent on time. But mostly we didn't see him. My mother never seemed to be angry with him, maybe because she just didn't have the energy, or maybe because she had the three of us kids to worry about.

Mom was confined to the one tiny, dim bedroom at the front of the apartment and a metal hospital bed kindly left behind by the Dominican Sisters (the bed became the couch after Mom died). She had a spoon hanging on a string from the bed and she'd use all her strength to knock the spoon against the metal frame to scare away mice or call for Camille. She kept her purse under her pillow and never spoke above a whisper. I had to position my ear very close to her mouth to hear her speak, but I confess I generally failed to follow her instructions. I hardly ever went to school, for instance.

I preferred to hang around Jefferson Park with one eye out for the truant officer. Like other hardcore truants, I had a system for keeping my parents in the dark about my attendance record: I used a pair of tweezers to extract the school's "cut slips" through the daisy window on the locked mailbox door. I thought I was doing the right thing, taking the long view. By my logic, I was going to be a New York Yankee; what good was school going to do me? At-bats were what I needed.

Once in a while, some of us would carry Mom downstairs in her wheelchair on a weekend afternoon so she could sit on the sidewalk in the sunshine and watch the world go by. When I saw someone drop a dollar bill into her lap, I thought for a serious minute about putting a "Please Help" sign inside my cap by her chair on the sidewalk, but I knew it would make her cry. Maybe I did it once or twice; it pains me even to try to recall. The humiliations of those days were so many. I was so young and it takes time to learn about morality in even the coziest of childhoods.

On that afternoon, Mom's disability offered an edge that, however distasteful, could allow me to feast on pizza and candy for a week. Edges, improved chances, are the stock in trade for a high-performance salesperson. I was, then as now, ever alert to moneymaking opportunities—though I do remember missing one big one. That was the time I got hold of, (1) a Bell & Howell movie projector my father had bought in better times, and (2) some porn films belonging a neighbor kid's father or uncle. We got the idea to project the movies out the window onto the building across the street just as the old ladies left the Bingo parlor. Their shrieks were priceless, but in retrospect we realized that we could have made serious change showing the movies in my apartment. Sometimes fun is a better reward than money. Everybody knows that!

My beautiful dark-haired, dark-eyed sister Camille—who everybody agreed was a prettier version of the heartthrob Italian-American singer, Connie Francis—cared for our mother and the rest of the family with almost no relief for 14 years, much of the time while also working the night shift as a telephone operator in midtown, near Grand Central Station. Camille had no childhood, none, and she nearly didn't survive it. But that's her story to tell.

Among a hundred other things, Camille was our main source of entertainment. We and all the neighbors called her Lucy, comparing her to crazy Lucille Ball, especially in that episode where Lucy has a job putting cherries into chocolates on an assembly line and everything gets out of control. Camille was always overwhelmed and having to improvise—using a bath towel for a tablecloth, that sort of thing—and always with a brave smile. We certainly had no money to go to the movies, and our cheap black and white television set was nicknamed Alaska because the screen was so snowy you could hardly make out the picture. A cockroach unlucky enough to squeeze into the back of the set only to be fried on one of the red-hot cathode ray tubes within was therefore called a Baked Alaska.

Camille was every bit as creative in her bid for all of us to survive as I was, particularly in her approach to discipline. Over and over I saw her choose to do the right thing even when that was the most difficult thing, to say no to her own needs and desires so that I could have or do something. She did everything she could, not only to keep me laughing, but also to keep me inside the apartment after dark, when she was working the midtown switchboard. In those days, the big hotels in Manhattan still had to place calls through a central operator. Whenever Camille got a celebrity dialer, especially a ball player, she poured on the charm and asked politely if they wouldn't mind speaking with her little brother *before* she completed their call! The possibility that someone like Mickey Mantle might call (he hung up on me) was often enough to keep me indoors at night; I always knew which ballplayers were in town. The Mets' Donn Clendon also hung up on me, and so did Sal Mineo, but there were two players on Sparky Anderson's Big Red Machine from Cincinnati, the pitcher Clay Carroll and the outfielder Bernie Carbo, destined to be a superstar, who took a shine to me and my brother and had us out to Shea Stadium for every game the Reds played against the Mets that year. We sat with the players' families and I felt so self-conscious about my duct-taped clothes and shoes and glasses that I did my best to clean up. Ultimately, I stopped going. I just couldn't stand to sit there looking as I did.

Every bit as much as I adored my big sister, I idolized my big brother Vinny. I dogged him everywhere he went, and I fed on his passion for Yankee history and stats. Vinny was handsome, with an air of movie star danger—sculpted black hair, blue eyes, and perfect features—that stood in contrast to his mild manner. He was the local stickball champion, a thrilling "three-sewer man"—meaning he could whack a pink rubber high-bounce ball, the famous Spalding (properly pronounced Spall-DEEN) the length of a city block. Vinny was so incredibly shy that he would routinely hide under the bed (or in the too-big-for-their-apartment cedar chest we got from the son-in-law of the Alibertis down the hall) to *avoid* the girls who followed him home, to my regular benefit (more on this later). In later years, I came to appreciate that Vinny spent far more energy developing my baseball skills than his own considerable talent, saving money he made working in the printing department at Lord & Taylor to buy me gloves and bats and such.

On my most self-pitying days, I actually used to think I had it rougher than my brother and sister because I had never even seen Mom walk and had known only poverty and chaos. I didn't have many good memories to draw upon. And I knew that Camille and Vinny were heartbreakingly obliged to place their time and most of their hope for the future in me. They were sufficiently older than me to serve as substitute parents and, like good parents, they were willing to sacrifice for my benefit. But really, they were just kids, overwhelmed, ill-attended kids who had so little to begin with that it was impossible for them, purely by virtue of self-sacrifice, to break the cycle of poverty and despair in which we lived. In truth, the only thing my brother and sister possessed to sacrifice for my benefit was their dreams. I'll always be grateful to them.

Vinny had dreamed of going to college. He even went so far as to enroll at Bronx Community, but he never attended a day of classes. I was in the room when Dad told Vinny he had to leave college to get a job and help pay for a home health aide to be there when the

Dominican Sisters were not, now that Camille had gotten married. Camille's good thing put additional pressure on Vinny, but he was so happy for her, he was never angry with her, just with the situation. I remember how crushed he was by Dad's words. His silent acquiescence was heart-rending and he never pursued that dream again, or any other. Instead, he became even more attached to the hope that my major league success would bail us out. Hope, however, pays no bills. I don't put much stock in hope.

Vinny was a great brother and he died too soon, just 60 years old, a doorman in a brass-buttoned suit in a nondescript building south of Gramercy Park in Manhattan. He was much beloved by the building residents and the circle of friends he maintained from the old neighborhood. We all miss him.

With little actual time to spend with us, my father, Carmine Belli, took a creative approach to our discipline. Because of his multiple jobs, he knew he had to tolerate a certain amount of craziness from us kids—boys—simply because he couldn't be there to do anything about it. In all honesty, he admired our spunk, our creativity. Dad was a nice-looking man, with a dark complexion and an early shock of gray hair. Never an athlete, he nevertheless encouraged both his sons in their pursuit of major league stardom in the can't-hurt way that people buy lottery tickets. Dad was not a churchgoing man, either, and didn't give us grief about all the girls visiting the apartment, so long as no one got pregnant, which, miraculously, no one did. Dad would begin whistling as soon as he came into the tenement hallway and before he started to ascend the stairs, loud enough for us to hear him and giving us maybe 45 seconds to disengage before he came through the apartment door. His family was all up in the Bronx, in Morris Park, and of little help to us from day to day, though we did go up and visit them sometimes. We called it "going to the country."

Although my mother came from a huge family of 16 children, only one of her siblings, Carmella, regularly helped us out. I don't know why she was the only one. Probably the best answer is that the rest of the family was scattered around East Harlem and struggling too, to put it mildly. My mother's mother had serious mental issues and a potty mouth that only became more and more embarrassing for everyone the older she got. I had cousins and in-laws on her side who were locked up, institutionalized, in gangs, on drugs, you name it. There were no drugs or crime in the Carmine Belli household, however, I assure you. There were plenty of teenaged girls and shadowy characters, but no drugs or crime. Remember the thousand eyes I said our father had on us? We never knew when we were being ratted out at a distance, and we knew where our father drew the line.

For instance, Mom had a sister who worked at John's Bargain Store and was always offering to throw a few extra things in the bag for us without ringing them up. My parents never allowed it. That set an example for us kids. If my father didn't give me a quarter or a dollar in the morning, I didn't ask why, I just carried on the best I could. We never stole. We asked, we cajoled, we pretended, we cried, we denied, we borrowed (we repaid), we went without. We made do. In truth, I'd say we welcomed the constraints demanded by morality—they placed some limit on the chaos and let us know that in some desperate way we were loved.

My Dad's mother would sometimes make the two-bus trip down from the Bronx on Sunday, bringing dinner, maybe even a homemade pizza. She spoke very little English but she was loaded with radar (thanks, Grandma!) and always found ways to make herself completely understood. For example, Grandma didn't like this one gal, a social worker who'd become infatuated with Vinny. So Grandma served her a plate of spaghetti topped with two meatballs and a sausage link arranged so as to leave no doubt she knew what was going on between them. She always made her point.

For years my Aunt Carmella appeared at our apartment door with a few groceries after working the night shift at the phone company (Carmella helped Camille get a job there, too). Our immediate next-door neighbor, Mary Aliberti, was also incredibly kind to my mother. She was a single mom and a super-old-school Italian. She and my mother were about the same age and Mary had plenty of her own hardships; she was living in East Harlem, too, after all. But Mary attended to my mother's every need when my sister was unavailable. I've never gotten over the sight of it: a stranger voluntarily cleaning my mother's urine bag and bedpan. After a sponge bath,

Mary would fix Mom's hair, help her put some lipstick on, encourage her to look at her pretty face in the mirror. Her compassion made a lasting impression on me. Her son, Sam, was also kind-hearted. For instance, he bought me a pair of gloves one day so I could get into a big snowball fight in progress, one of countless generosities by the Aliberti family towards me, and a quality that left a lasting impression.

Any act of generosity makes both people feel good and that's reason enough to do it. That's not generosity's only reward, however, because generosity isn't limited to gifts of material things. When you share such things as time, attention, and wisdom, you assume the role of a teacher. In so doing, you gain clarity about your own work; you become better at what you do simply by taking the time to explain it. It's a form of practice not much different from fielding grounders. The best business people I've ever worked with were tremendously generous with their time, their experience, and their ideas. Generosity is a defining trait of the Street-Smart salesman.

Too few people appreciate the personal rewards of generosity, however. You'd think that maybe some neighbors would come by our place with the leftover ziti, but it isn't true. Everybody was poor. Most of our neighbors were doing better than we were only because they were healthy. Near the end, when Mom went into the chronic-care facility at St. Barnabas in the Bronx and Camille got married, our bad situation grew even worse. If things were a mess with two women in the house, you can imagine what a mess it became with just my father, brother, and me.

As much as Camille and Vinny did for me and for Mom, I—the cute, talented, and ever-innovative baby of the family—could do no wrong. I was precocious and charming and wielded unexpected authority. As I got older, I pretty much ruled the family with my scheming and treasure hunting, always finding my own creative ways to get what I, or the family, needed.

Once when I was 10 years old, for instance, I was sitting on the stoop with Vinny when our landlord, Mr. Wilkes, came by, grumbling about needing a new super for the building. I volunteered my brother and me to be the supers for a fee of $42 a month, the same amount as our rent, and maybe as much money as I could conceive of having. "You want to be the supers so you don't have to pay rent?" he asked. Hmmm. I decided to go for the gold. "Charge Dad for the rent, same as always, and pay us our own $42," I said, never thinking he would actually agree. Cheap bastard that he was, he said okay. Who hires a 10-year-old, even one with a big brother, to be the superintendent of a six-story building?

"Martinez on the fifth floor has no water," he said. So we went up there with some tools and not a single idea of what to do. We ripped the sink out of the wall. That was fun, but not educational. The problem became worse. So we went down to the basement, like superintendents do. We poked around in the moldy dark, wrenches and hammers in hand, and made more of a mess, something along the lines of *The Three Stooges*. In a few hours, we were itching with flea bites and on our way to Harlem Hospital emergency room again. It wasn't unusual for the water to be off in our tenement for days or weeks at a time, so we waited a whole week before we called Wilkes from the pay phone on the corner to tell him that, after much investigation, we had determined that the Martinez problem required the services of a *real* plumber. The beauty of it all was that I convinced Wilkes to pay us for one week's services, a full 15 dollars.

Another time, a beauty from across the street, also in love with Vinny, remarked that her mother needed the apartment painted. Again, I suggested we were the boys for the job. This time I asked for a hundred dollars to do the job. I gave $15 each to two Puerto Rican newcomers, Cheyo and his friend, to do the actual painting, and kept $70 for myself in my capacity as painting inspector. That small business lasted through five apartments—until baseball season came again.

I was always doing my best to beat the deck stacked against us. I did the best I could to keep our apartment safe, too. An old, unrepentant alcoholic we took to calling Uncle Steve began coming by every afternoon to drink a quart of Rheingold beer and smoke Pall Malls in our kitchen. Steve must have been in his mid-forties at the time, harmless to others, his own worst enemy. I loved him because he was there every day and because he seemed to care about my brother and me. It didn't take much to earn my affection back then.

Uncle Steve may have been a drunk, but he had a big heart and his simple presence made me feel safe. In general, addicts, thieves, pushers, prostitutes, and wiseguys had the run of the hallways and the streets around my building: Just to have an adult male around the apartment, even a drunk like Uncle Steve, made it less likely that we'd be robbed of what little we had—or beaten up for having nothing to steal after they'd gone through all the trouble of breaking in.

We hardly ever ate a cooked meal: The stove was full of roaches that fled in droves when you turned on the heat. We owned no pots and pans, no dishes or glasses that weren't cracked and chipped. After the handle broke on the refrigerator, Uncle Steve put a padlock on it. He didn't actually lock it, but it wouldn't have mattered. There wasn't much inside anyway.

If there happened to be a supermarket special on olives, we'd get five cans and stab at the tops with a screwdriver when we were hungry (the can opener lost years before had never been replaced). Mostly, I ate Yankee Doodles or Devil Dogs (breakfast and anytime), washed down either with Pepsi or a Manhattan Special, a super-sweet black coffee soda I think was actually made in Brooklyn. I considered a slice of pizza a full meal, and tiny steamed White Castle hamburgers were a delicacy.

As a consequence of my nearly all-sugar diet and general lack of hygiene, I lost almost all my teeth while I was still a kid. I never saw a dentist until President Johnson established the Medicaid program and I went to Golden's dental clinic on 125th and Lexington Avenue. On my first visit there I was found to have 32 cavities. Adult humans have 32 teeth, so you do the math. The dentist put me to sleep without telling me what was going to happen, then pulled four—count 'em, *four*—of my front teeth. I completely freaked out when I woke up from the anesthetic, and I made myself scarce for approximately six months, skulking, hiding my mouth behind a dirty handkerchief. My neighbors were pretty sure I'd become a junkie. My teachers thought I'd gone hysterically mute from all the craziness in our family. And all girls thought, correctly in my view, that I was a big-time loser.

Girls had more reason to regard me harshly than my toothlessness, I'll confess. Remember I mentioned that Vinny was so shy he'd hide under the bed to avoid his would-be girlfriends? Well, sometimes one or another bombshell would follow him home and, by prior agreement, I'd pretend that Vinny wasn't home. He'd hide and they'd almost always decide to wait for him. After a while, they'd get tired of waiting and turn their eye to me. I therefore had a lot of action, enough to be the envy of any teen, especially for a 12-year-old. It wasn't lost on me, then as now, that you don't have to have to be first pick to go home a winner. You don't even have to have all the goods; you just have to have a strategy! Sometimes just *being in the room* is a strategy. I had more girlfriends than anybody I knew, no matter what their age.

Actually, now that I think of it, even in my toothless stage, there was a girl uptown I had my eye on. I remember

sitting in a car with her, whimpering behind a handkerchief, letting her do the talking. I scored that day too, and
it was one of many incidents in my childhood that led to
another Street-Smart understanding—that it's sometimes
best to keep your mouth shut in order to achieve an end.

For example, take the afternoon of July 5 back in the
early 1960s. My cousin had come down from the Bronx
with some leftover fireworks—Roman candles, ash cans,
punks, firecrackers—and a box of matches. I threw a lit
firecracker out the back window into the yard and that was
fun, so I threw another. This time a lit piece of firecracker
paper drifted back in the window and settled onto the
pile of fireworks on the floor. The whole pile exploded
and the apartment caught fire. Vinny and Camille carried
our mother out to the street. The Fire Department and
NYPD arrived, but I was more concerned about what
my father was going to do than about the firemen and
cops. To the extent the cops cared, they interrogated
me down at Harlem Hospital, where I was treated for
burns. "You know anything about how this fire started?"
they asked me. Not a word from my mouth. Somehow, I
guess because the fire didn't spread, the whole question of
responsibility went away. What remained was water stains,
smoke damage, and rocket burns in the ceiling—and the
notion that it's sometimes most productive just to keep
your mouth shut.

I wore the same clothes every day. I had one jacket,
one shirt, one pair of pants, one pair of underwear, one
pair of socks, one pair of duct-taped sneakers and one pair
of duct-taped eyeglasses with an outdated prescription.

We used a lot of duct tape. One of Dad's jobs made big use of the stuff, and we always had several big rolls around the apartment that we used to fix everything: We taped our baseball bats and balls with it; we *made* baseballs with it. I also used it for decoration, putting Mantle's number 7 not only on the front door but on the back of my mother's new wheelchair.

When I was eight years old, I suggested to Camille, who was slightly bow-legged, that we duct-tape her legs together to straighten them. It was a hot summer day, and as sure as we were that it would work, we didn't know how long it would take. After two hours in the sweltering heat, the glue on the tape melted onto her skin and wouldn't come off. Back to the emergency room we went.

Much as I'd like to, I'm unable to forget the day I got pulled from my homeroom class at Benjamin Franklin High School and sent to see the guidance counselor. There, in his office, I was informed that I had become "a distraction" to my teachers and other students. I remember thinking that that was odd because I slept through most of the school day. Then he lowered the boom, as quickly and directly as possible. "Mr. Belli, you smell," he announced. I could not respond! To think I'd been feeling so embarrassed about my missing teeth when all the time I was stinking up the room in addition to being perpetually sick and hungry and carrying a monumental chip on my shoulder. Okay, I knew it was time for a shower, but where? *I didn't own a toothbrush.* I don't remember that I got cleaned up that day, either. I don't think I did. I just lived with an enhanced sense of shame that can still sting.

I'd estimate I visited the emergency room at Harlem Hospital at least once a month. Colds, viruses, headaches, earaches, stitches, rashes, toothaches, dizziness—all were regular complaints. I spent countless hours in the ER waiting for my name to be called, feeling invisible. A desire to be looked upon with something other than pity or derision took me over pretty quickly. I needed to be admired, recognized, commended, for my ability to do something positive. It was as simple as that. I was always finding little ways to distinguish myself. Yankee star was everyone's prediction for me, and as sole possessor of a possible big future in my battered family, I was always the best ballplayer I could possibly be. Everyone around me seemed as sure (to a 10-year-old boy) as a person could be that I would one day wear the beloved uniform. So I put a lot of time into that.

I'm always aware of time, most specifically the time it takes to do something versus what you reap from the time spent. I'm no procrastinator, not even a little bit. I sometimes flash on the memory of a kid from my school, the teacher's pet, an altar boy type who was always being bullied, but always said hello to me. One afternoon, he said hello again as he passed by my stoop, and a minute later he was dead, murdered in a botched hold-up at the candy store on First Avenue. Despite the fact that I was seeing people get shot left and right all the time, I couldn't get over the shock of that boy's death when I heard. I might even say that the shock of it is one of the reasons why I bring a strong sense of urgency to everything that I do.

Today, though, I have a beautiful wife, Marian, whom I met when I was 14 years old on a trip to "the country," the Bronx. Marian's family lived across the street from Dad's sister, Rose. I thought Marian McKenna's big Irish family was loaded because they had food in the refrigerator *and* all wore nice, clean clothes. She wasn't rich, just middle class, although rich in spirit. She had an affection for strays, including me, that she has to this day. She'd take the train down to Harlem a few times a week, with cake or clothes or just wearing a new dress, and stay for a few hours for some poor folks' entertainment. We married when I was a junior in college and she was already working at the electric company, Consolidated Edison. We had two cats before Marian recently began studying to be a veterinary technologist after retiring from Con Ed (we now have four cats).

Marian has a great heart and soul and she has been my Number 1 cheerleader for more than 40 years—never underestimate the sustaining power of someone else's belief in you. Very often, a friend, loved one, coach, teacher, or other elder, believes in you long before you do. That's because their experience tells them something about you that you are too naive to understand. If you have someone who believes in you and you do your best to deliver a level of effort consistent with their expectations, you likely will find that their faith in you was not misguided. Conversely, if you get the chance to be a mentor, take it. You win either way. It's another of the rewards of generosity.

2

The Million-Dollar Accident

Luck is the residue of design.

—Branch Rickey

Everybody gets into sales by accident. In 30-plus years as a salesman, I've never met anybody, *ever*, who said they took a sales job because they wanted to be a salesperson, much less because they saw sales as their first step toward making a million dollars. Very few, *too* few, people see the wealth-building potential of a career in sales. I'd estimate that fully half the people who ever take a sales job do so out of sheer desperation, only to perform poorly and get out of the field fast and forever. Things were different with me.

In my case, I couldn't get a job as a gym teacher (as I'll explain, I managed to earn a college degree in Physical Education), so I took a job selling life insurance, you know, just to tide me over. My brother-in-law had bought a policy from a broker he liked who'd mentioned the company was looking for people, so I called and arranged for an interview. When I took that job with MetLife, I certainly had no idea that I'd changed my career trajectory forever and for the better. But before too long, I began to notice that I was better at selling life insurance than my middle-class counterparts, who often complained of having trouble "reading" their prospects. I, on the other hand, was dealing very effectively with my clients, making good use of my self-styled "ghetto radar"—I sold a million dollars worth of insurance in my first year!

A lifetime of navigating favors and figuring out whom to ask for what and when and how was suddenly paying off in hard cash. No one was more dumbfounded by my luck than I was. I was relieved that it had only taken me five years to get through college! My colleagues with middle-class family backgrounds appeared to be at something of a disadvantage in sales because, unlike me, they didn't doubt every story and promise they heard. *Their* personal experience suggested that people are generally truthful; mine suggests otherwise. But the ability to tell the truth from a lie is key to success in sales, mainly because customers always lie at least a little, and especially in the beginning. Lying is the way customers and prospects alike protect themselves from assumedly predatory sales-people.

Unlike most of the other entry-level salespeople, I possessed the enviable ability to conduct an unemotional analysis of a selling situation and, moreover, to predict individual behaviors. I was able to size up a prospect quickly, and with impressive accuracy, thereby increasing my rate of return. For the first time in my life, I appeared to have an advantage over the people around me. It was hard to believe, I'll admit, but the numbers were there to prove it.

It wasn't all clear sailing, of course. I had the ability to read a stranger, yes, but my otherwise complete and total lack of social skills set me apart from my colleagues in other, isolating, ways too. "Small talk" (I didn't even know the phrase) mystified me, and I sure didn't know how to do a single thing right in a restaurant setting. But even though I couldn't compete with my new colleagues on social terms, I took comfort in knowing that I had a nose for opportunity and gift for negotiating and deal making that was as good or better than anybody else's in the room, and that I was making better money.

I began to see myself as a diamond in the rough. I began to set short- then long-term goals and standards for myself and set them high; I wanted to replace the huge chip I'd been carrying on my shoulder with sky's-the-limit talent and ambition. As my successes mounted and I gained a working knowledge of socially acceptable behaviors, the chip on my shoulder felt lighter and lighter. I wouldn't say it's gone altogether now—do we ever leave our childhoods completely behind?—but it doesn't hinder me either.

Do you know what's interesting—and most encouraging—about things such as personality, intelligence, math ability, social and practical skills, educational degrees? None of them has proven definitive in predicting a person's success at sales—though in some cases, a higher level of education may be essential, depending on the complexity of the product. However, it is unethical and illegal to inquire into the personal history of a sales recruit, even though research has revealed such details to be the most reliable predictors of success.[1] I'm glad of that; I was certainly grateful not to have to answer any questions about my background, or I might never have gotten my foot in the door. Who would think such a shabby kid had the potential to bring in a million dollars in business his first year? That's why it's illegal and unethical to ask; we're all entitled to our shot.

Women now account for about a quarter of the national sales workforce,[2] but there was a time, not so long ago and not even entirely gone, when women were considered too emotional for the manly job of sales work and too prone to turnover (in the form of marriage, children) to be worth spending the money to train them. Similarly, it used to be thought that people wouldn't buy from a minority salesperson (the growing numbers of ethnic minority salespeople now suggests the contrary) and that older people don't have the energy for the job (though they may make up for lost footwork in experience and savvy). But I advise you not to waste energy lamenting the unfairness of affirmative action laws, hiring quotas, and the like. At base, a salesperson's job is to compete . . . with *anybody*.

When I say anybody, I mean anybody. I think this might be a good time for me to shed a little more light on the cast of characters around 416 East 119th Street, all of whom I needed to deal with as with productively as possible. Upstairs we had Ron (I've forgotten his last name if I ever knew it), an African-American gentleman who was said to have gone insane and lost his career and professional standing—how else to explain his living in the Italian part of Harlem? Poor thing did little more than count backwards from one hundred over and over and over, day and night. He often sat at the opposite end of our kitchen table from Uncle Steve. They made quite a pair. But like I said, their presence was a good hedge against break-ins. The Belli door had no lock and was otherwise undefended, you see. More on this later.

From elsewhere in the neighborhood, Mr. George M. Cruz, a fixture of our stoop who was homosexual, insisted on the middle initial and was completely in love with Vinny, though mercifully content just to bask in his glow. George would often sing dramatic *a cappella* ballads at the top of his lungs in my and my brother's honor. He had no discernable job, so he must have had an income from somewhere; maybe that's why he insisted on the middle initial, because he was living in diminished circumstances, as opposed to the rest of us, who knew no other.

Then there was Father Jim, a sort of itinerant Catholic priest doing time in a local parish, who dropped by most days all summer for three summers, ostensibly to advance the cause of our family's salvation, but also to drink until drunk, then sleep it off in the hospital bed (this was after Mom had gone into the nursing home). There was Dixie, the runaway I mentioned in the Introduction, from Holyoke, Massachusetts. Blonde, plump, pretty, kind, victimized. We looked the other way on the few occasions when she turned tricks in our apartment. Her gratitude for the roof we put over her head, damaged as it was, usually came back to us in the form of giggles and sandwiches. She disappeared for weeks at a time, and finally forever.

There was a numbers runner for the Mob we'd allow to leave bags of cash in the apartment for short periods of time. We were offered money in exchange for our welcome mat, but we never, ever took it; that would have been crossing the line. Sex and drinking was one thing, but Dad drew the line at consorting with junkies and criminals and so did we, in our way. We figured it was good for the numbers runner to owe us favors because nothing kept an apartment safe like word that the Mob was watching the door. Believe me, currency does not always take the form of dollars. Having a local wiseguy looking out for you was solid gold.

There actually was one junkie who sometimes hung around our place. Vinny used to think that he robbed other apartments and brought whatever he got to our door, like some kind of junkie Robin Hood. But in truth, the guy didn't have to steal to support his habit. His mother gave him money for heroin, just so that he didn't have to steal and worse. This was a woman with the ability to prioritize! Nobody in those days had ever heard of anybody who had kicked heroin; there was no treatment back then. Anyway, he didn't bring dangerous lowlifes around. Mostly he was just getting in from the rain.

I became a serious student of human behavior, and, extreme as all these characters were, they have much more in common with the rest of humanity than you might think: habits, quirks, troubles, aspirations, delusions. In dealing with them effectively I learned many things, including to be patient and keep my trap shut when I had a secret to keep or knew nothing useful, to be humble and inquisitive enough to ask for help and advice when I needed it, and how to direct a conversation to my benefit. Confronting chaos at every turn, I came to understand that I needed *to know as much about a situation as I possibly could before I made any move.*

I remember a time, for instance, when I was hanging out with some guys talking about a hot girl one of them was able to describe in great detail. I remember how close I came to echoing his words, because I knew the gal he was talking about. It was a good thing I didn't, but I sensed a physical mood change among the other guys in the room. She turned out to be the wife of one of them, who went home, beat her up, then came back to club the poor soul who had his eye on her. You better believe I made a mental note to watch my words forevermore.

I had hungry eyes and ears, not just belly, and I was always making mental notes of everything happening around me. I could switch tactics on a dime, too. Sometimes I think that the biggest difference between my childhood and my professional life is that as a professional I have time to plan, not always have to be flying by the seat of my pants—though I certainly can!

In a manner I found strangely luxurious, once I started to have some success as a salesman, I began to manage my professional time in minutes and hours—as opposed to weeks, months, and years—because small successes are the foundation for larger ones. I also began to develop my own paper-and-pen information systems. I remain—never mind the phone at my ear or computer in my hand—a major fan of the index card. There's nothing like a small space to focus the mind. I further refined my craft by reading books about business, economics, and philosophy, and by attending sales training seminars on my own time and dime. The sharp eye that let me distinguish a change-up from a slider was now laser-focused on my bottom line with a simple overarching goal: to make a million dollars, the non-millionaire's magic number. But how does a total non-millionaire like me come up with and carry out a plan that would make him such a fortune?

■　■　■

Of course, a dream is not a plan, but a plan can arise from a dream if the dream is taken on as a *goal*. Like a dream, a plan is free to have. A poor person can dream up a plan just the same as anyone. If I started with a goal, I reasoned, and worked backwards from there to the smaller objectives I'd have to meet today, tomorrow, next week, month, year, in order to achieve a certain result, I couldn't fail. That was a very comforting thought to me. I knew another thing for sure too: You can't wait for the perfect moment to get started on a mission. Any moment will do.

Here's the story of my very first long-term plan. A harsh reality dawned on me back in the summer of 1969, when I went to see the Democratic candidate for mayor of New York City, fellow Italian-American Mario Proccacino, at a street-corner rally at 116th Street and First Avenue, a few blocks from our apartment. I remember the candidate as well dressed, and the promises he made as thrilling, dramatic. Speaking from a platform in the middle of the intersection, Proccacino said he had a plan to clear the neighborhood of junkies, winos, hookers, and dope dealers, and to rebuild the decaying and burned out buildings all around us. Sounded good to me.

But after Mario headed back downtown in his limo and I had threaded my way back to our apartment through the bigger than usual crazy crowd, I found myself taking a rare, clear-eyed inventory of our dreary kitchen. I saw with cruel clarity that Mario Proccacino and the city government were not going to get me the hell out of our kitchen, much less East Harlem, at least not without plenty of help from me. I thought of all the brief visits from social workers we'd ever had. Many of them were well meaning, but after an hour they were gone, all their forms filled in, and you were on your own again. They'd been coming around as long as I could remember. Now, though, I was 16 years old. I had to get control of my destiny, and pronto. Flushed with mounting anxiety, I promised myself right then and there that I'd start going to school every day. As I said, you gotta start somewhere. The idea of my having a perfect attendance record had all the allure of the impossible.

This was not the first time I'd been touched by fear of failure, of course. Academics presented me with the highest potential for failure of anything I could imagine; this was not going to be easy. It had taken a whole lot of finagling for me to get into high school in the first place. When I was in the eighth grade, you see, I flunked several subjects and was ordered to attend summer school. I didn't attend summer school though, because summer is for baseball. When August rolled around and I had to retake the same tests I'd flunked in the spring, my scores were even lower. Panic set in. I had to go to high school!

I went to the convent next door to my school, Holy Rosary. I knocked on the door and asked for my Sister, and remained standing outside. Moments later, she opened the door a crack. Let me first say that Sister regarded me as a sorry-case kid on a fast track to prison. I knew she was wrong about this, but I didn't go to school often enough to convince her. Anyway, as far as I could tell—and I'm sure she wouldn't have agreed—Sister cut me no slack whatsoever. So I did what I had to do: cried real tears and used my mom's declining condition to give me an excuse for not showing up and her to give me a diploma. I promised her I'd go to school every day. She listened for maybe half a minute, then closed the door, without a word. I stood there and waited for what seemed like another summer. Then, the door opened again, a little wider this time, and Sister reappeared, now with a rolled-up piece of paper in her hand. My diploma! She couldn't bring herself to hand it to me, though. Instead, she threw it past me, over my head into the gutter and closed the door, again, without a word.

Good enough. I scooped up that damp scroll as an excellent infielder should, proud of the fact that using whatever irresistible combination of nerve, charm, good looks, athleticism (I'd impressed the school in that way at least), and drawing on the deep well of sympathy for my anguished family, I'd charmed my way to a diploma.

But I didn't maintain my focus on school attendance and now I was 16 years old. I'd been suspended three times from the only high school that had accepted me, a trade school called the New York High School of Printing. My infractions were three: one for sending a mash note, signed Alfonso Capone, to a teacher, a leggy gal who regularly wore fishnet stockings in contrasting colors to her skirt; what was I to think? The second was for throwing my bat in frustration; it landed too near the coach. Well, maybe it hit him. The last straw was for some shenanigans in math class having to do with the somewhat deaf but, more importantly, incredibly slow-moving teacher. She would turn to write on the blackboard, and I, with this other guy, Carlos, would move her desk out into the hall. Amazing how long it would take her to notice that anything had happened. Note to self: There are such people.

Then I got thrown out of Printing and sent to Ben Franklin in East Harlem. I made a new pact with myself to go to school every day. My grades didn't go up but my attendance did, and that was when things first started to turn around. It was how I first came to understand that in the world beyond our apartment, *showing up* is key to getting ahead. If nobody can see you, nobody can notice you—and nobody can spot your talent(s) and take you under their wing.

Once I'd established a solid attendance record, I went to see the high school guidance counselor to see if he could help me get into a college, any college. I wasn't expecting there was much he could do for me, but I had to ask. Talk about brazen. To my utter amazement and eternal gratitude, he proceeded to tell me about a new scholarship program at the City College of New York (CCNY) in West Harlem called SEEK, which stood for "Search for Education, Elevation and Knowledge." SEEK covered full tuition and expenses for "economically disadvantaged and academically unprepared" students such as me, and it is still in operation today. "Academically unprepared!" We used to say that the only requirement for SEEK was that you be *breathing*. I got in.

Many years later, in 2007, I endowed the SEEK program's first private scholarship.

The Street-Smart Seven!

- To have a dream is pointless without both a plan and the willingness to execute.
- Treat selling as a *profession*, not a job.
- Be a serious student of human behavior.
- People lie a little, but prospects lie a lot!
- Know as much as you possibly can about a situation before making a move.
- Don't wait for the best time to get started on something important. There is no best time. Anytime will do.
- You have to be visible to be noticed. Be there. Show up!

3

Why Not Me?

Courage is resistance to fear, mastery of fear—not absence of fear.

—Mark Twain

Once I was admitted to SEEK at the City College of New York, instead of feeling on top of the world, I found myself consumed with a brand new fear. As one of several hundred college freshmen with fresh hope and deeply troubled childhoods, some abusive and many times worse than mine, I became worried that I would soon be exposed as the dumbest kid of them all, maybe even *of all time*. I fought not to surrender to my fear of the possibility that I might be an actual 100 percent idiot, unteachable and unemployable, doomed to spend the rest of my life angry and scavenging.

New fears will replace the old ones. As far as I can tell, that's a universal rule. Money, financial security, nothing buys freedom from fear, sorry to say. No one—*no one*—rich or poor, lives free from fear. The rich live better than the poor, without a doubt, but the rich have their fears, too—fears of being unloved, unappreciated, losing their money, sickness, loneliness, and death, in no particular order. The rich and the poor have at least that much in common. But the rich don't have to confront their fears all day, every day, as the poor do.

Poor people live with constant low-level fears subject to spike under various and sudden circumstances, as well as the kind of oppositional, double-edged fears that chip away at a person's self-image: fear of being invisible coupled with fear of being noticed; fear of failure paired with fear of success; fear of going home trumped by fear of having nowhere to go. The question, I have come to see, is how do we *harness* our fears? How do we use the abundant energy that feeds our doubts and suspicions to a better purpose?

Put to good use, fear can be a very powerful engine of change. Back in the 1960s, Mel Brooks and Carl Reiner had great success with a hilarious comedy routine called *The 2,000 Year Old Man*. Reiner was the straight man, the interviewer; Brooks was the elderly Jew who had lived through all of recorded history. "What was the main means of getting from place to place back in ancient times?" he is asked. The 2,000 year old man thinks for a moment and answers in a heavy comic accent, "Fear, mostly... An animal would growl at you and you would run two miles in a minute." Brooks always a got a big laugh with that answer, but let me tell you, he was telling the truth. Fear was certainly my constant companion. In the best scenarios, I could hold fear at bay, in the shadows, but it took every ounce of my nerve and creativity to do it.

Having found myself just one among hundreds of hard cases, all I could think of to keep myself from being overwhelmed by self-doubt was to work harder than anyone else, to bring the discipline and drive I brought to baseball to my schoolwork. That was all, but it turned out to be enough. In the beginning, I was very, very careful not to set my goals too high. I wanted to get some achievement under my belt at this stage, to prove I wasn't the dumbest, worst student in the history of the SEEK program. I spent the whole first year taking daily remedial classes to bring my eighth-grade level reading, writing, and math skills up to college entry level. Being in the company of so many determined grammatically and arithmetically challenged students made significant improvement possible on my part, even easy, because the embarrassment quotient was eliminated.

I remember one teacher in particular, an African-American professor of English Literature. He was a big man, very articulate, with a big, deep voice. He seemed to have a dislike for the SEEK program in general and for wayward know-nothings like me in particular. He viewed SEEK as a handout that diminished his own accomplishments, and he flat-out called me a fraud, telling me, "I know how you got here, but you're not going to leave the same way," meaning I was going to have to *earn* my way to a college degree, that the one and only handout I'd ever received in life was now history. I took his anger to heart because I was ashamed of my circumstances and unsure of myself. But I hoped he was right about me in one important way, that I possessed the capacity to learn.

Nevertheless, because I couldn't fully appreciate the strengths my teachers identified in me, I remained prey to the idea that people in authority were scheming to humiliate me. At some point, I took the Intro Psych course, for which I wrote a term paper about my personal theory on the relationship between poverty and achievement—I wish I still had it so we could quote it here! When I received an invitation to the Psychology Department awards ceremony a few weeks later, I showed up mainly because the teacher had winked at me when she handed me the invite and I wanted to know what she'd meant. I thought—hoped—she was making a pass at me; I had no appreciation for the social taboos regarding teachers and students. At Benjamin Franklin High School, there'd been a kid we called One-Eyed Willie who wore a patch over his eye and enjoyed rock star status because he was rumored to be having sex with not one, but two, pretty hot teachers. I couldn't appreciate the appeal of the eye patch, but I did appreciate knowing that a defect doesn't have to be a disqualifier.

Anyway, I sat in the back of the auditorium the whole time, actively fighting the urge to flee. And when my name was called to receive the department award for Best Term Paper, I was so dizzy and lost in thought that all I heard was my name. Having my name called in class had never been a good thing before. So when everyone turned to look at me, applauding with their crazy-wide smiles, I became doubly, triply, home run certain there was a department-wide conspiracy afoot to mess with my head. I might even have turned around to look behind me to see who was being cheered. Somehow, I found my way to the front of the room, took the certificate in two shaking hands and escaped without further incident. Many hours passed, sitting—somewhere—by myself, staring at my name on the paper, before I fully comprehended that not only had I *passed* the psychology course, I had *excelled*. *Then* I understood what my teacher's wink had meant.

I began to set more ambitious goals for myself. Each time I met a goal I set another, slightly higher one; achievability was important. In the end, it took me five years to graduate instead of the usual four, but okay, I needed year one just for the Three Rs. Basically, by applying the work ethic I previously gave only to baseball, I earned a college degree with a major in Physical Education. On my way, I played varsity ball for CCNY, a Division I team, for four years, during which I took home three batting titles and two Most Valuable Player awards. In 1991, I was inducted into the CCNY Athletic Hall of Fame.

On college graduation day, I was all geared up to get some public school kids in shape, win some ball games, some championships, enjoy tenure, summers off, and a good pension. Where I come from, a civil service job is synonymous with easy street. My future looked bright at last. But it turned out there were no jobs for Physical Education teachers in mid-1970s New York. So I did what so many do: I deferred my dream and took an entry-level job to tide me over. I'd be selling life insurance.

The Street-Smart Seven!

- Fears demand energy that may be put to much better use. Fear can be a very powerful engine of change.

- When you harness fears, you can redirect the energy that fed them to fuel yourself for other challenges.

- Sometimes all you can do to keep self-doubt at bay is work harder than anyone else. That's a good response! More specific goals will come.

- Don't set short-term goals too high; make them achievable. Meeting one target recharges your energy for the next.

- Don't be afraid to lose; just don't embrace defeat.

(continued)

(continued)

- A defect, a shortcoming, doesn't have to be a disqualifier.
- New fears will replace the old ones. No one lives free of fear. In fact, some form of fear motivates most people. Factor this understanding into your life and work.

4

Your Advantage Is That No One Takes You Seriously

> A common mistake that people make is to underestimate the ingenuity of complete fools.
>
> —Douglas Adams

I am well aware that everyone makes fun of salespeople. Americans love to feel sorry for us. I attribute this national disdain to every American highschooler's being forced to read Arthur Miller's play, *Death of a Salesman*, with its exhausted central character, Willie Loman, struggling for love and meaning as his sales numbers go down.

He's hardly a role model, but whether we salespeople like it or not, Willie Loman is who most Americans think of when you tell them what you do for a living; they can't imagine living with such uncertainty themselves. Personally, I laugh it off. I'm able to laugh because in my life's journey people have assumed much worse things of me than that I was a loser. Plus, I'm living a life I love, entirely free from financial anxiety even in the current dreadful economy.

I am also well aware that nobody trusts salespeople. Because they assume we are desperate, they further assume that we are somehow cheating them. Like ambulance chasers (aka lawyers), salespeople score little higher in the popular estimation than thieves and liars. Let me assure you, however, that the vast majority of the millions of sales transactions that take place across this country and around the world every day are completely above board and satisfactory to all parties involved. If you think this is a book about how to scam your customers using my wily secrets, you're wrong. The truth, as we'll see, is that most salespeople are honest and it's *customers* who lie!

Businesses need services and supplies to keep things running. People need milk, shoes, furniture and, yes, insurance. Schools need pencils, doctors need tongue depressors, trucks need tires. Sales are the engine of the national economy and salespeople start it up and salesforces keep it running. A sales career can take good care of you all your life. You want job security? Become a high-performance salesperson. In a 2004 compensation survey conducted by a monthly trade publication, the average income for a sales rep across American industry was $111,135, calculated as a base salary of $70,588 plus $40,547 in bonuses and commissions and I would assert these numbers are higher today despite the sluggish economy.[1] The textbook I used for teaching my business students asserted that college graduates who go straight into sales tend to make better money than other nascent professionals and, because of the direct correlation between performance and compensation in the field, are fully able to keep pace with other professionals over the course of their careers.[2]

A few years ago, in addition to my sales work, I began teaching business courses at Mercy College in Dobbs Ferry, New York, not far from my home. As a visiting professor, I taught classes in economics, consumer behavior, marketing, and sales management. Most of my students came from working-class families in the greater New York area.

Often, I would ask a roomful of students, "Who wants to be a millionaire?" Every hand in the room would go up. Then I'd ask who thought he or she has what it takes to become a millionaire. That's when 90 percent of the hands would go down. And they *should* go down, because most people don't have the drive and discipline to make—build—a fortune.

I believe that's because most Americans are reconciled to the idea that they'll never be rich. Moreover, I believe they can live with this diminished view of their potential only because they were never poor. They don't know what it's like at the bottom of the heap, so they don't fear it; they think poverty only happens to poor people. These are the same people who buy lottery tickets, mind you, on the chance that they'll hit a big payday. Could happen! But the enemy of great is good. I say stop playing Lotto and start betting on *you*.

Like millions around the world, I was entranced by the movie *Slumdog Millionaire*. Unlike anybody I knew, however, I saw myself in the dirt-poor protagonist. The significant difference between his and my story, of course, is that mine is real and his is fiction. The story I'm telling here endeavors to show how a person can apply the lessons of misfortune toward the creation of financial wealth; his story hinged on extraordinary good fortune, namely that the questions asked of him were questions to which he, a totally uneducated boy, knew the answers, up to and including the name of a lesser character in a nineteenth century French novel. The slumdog didn't *make* his luck, though it was suggested in a sentimental way that love, intelligence, and persistence played ineffable roles in his success. Perhaps they did. But what I saw was a fairy tale character who was the beneficiary of eight consecutively perfect twists of fate, an output of good fortune that I don't have to tell you rarely occurs in real life, much less in my classroom.

What I also saw, in the character of the game show host, was a person with all the hallmarks of an East Harlem con man, a slick-looking, smooth-talking phony with a big, broad smile. The kind of guy who always has an answer and, for that reason alone, is not to be trusted. We'll talk more about this later, but when someone puts you strongly in mind of someone else, take it seriously.

My students were taking college-level business courses because they either hoped or meant—there's a big difference—to live their lives free of financial anxiety. They were middle-class kids who'd grown up with the resources and expectations of family, friends, schools, and religious institutions. Most of them—and likely you, too—didn't realize that the slick host of the television show deliberately gave the slumdog the wrong answer to the million-rupee question. They imagined that the self-important emcee would reveal himself to have a generous heart, perhaps having seen something of himself in this street urchin poised between bliss and oblivion. They couldn't imagine what trouble could come of the host's making sure this beloved underdog captured the prize. I sure could. I considered all the angles.

There's a single overarching reason why the emcee would never for a second consider helping our hero: *There's nothing in it for him.* He would never be able to take credit for his kindness, and credit is all a spokesman gives and takes. Heaven forbid the kid someday let it slip about the tip—the emcee's credibility would be gone on the breeze—and a spokesperson is nothing without his good name.

Of course, the puffed-up host had good reason to believe the boy would keep quiet forever: No one is quick to admit that he cheated on a test. Because it wasn't the emcee's story, the script never considered what would have happened if he'd been discovered to have given the *wrong* answer to the boy, as he actually did. What if the boy, shocked at the betrayal, had stood and denounced him on the spot? In my experience, there were lots of reasons not to trust this shill.

What I ask you to do is to *look deeply* into people and situations. *Take your time.* Study, analyze, and consider. There is so much information freely available, and so much you don't appreciate that you already know. What the slumdog hero did was *extrapolate* the correct answer based on everything he knew about the wider world—knowledge gained in moments of truth and moments of laughter, in glimpses and glances and overheard conversations. Everything he'd ever experienced, no matter how accidental, turned out to be important. That's the romance of that plot twist: We are eager to believe that everything that happens to us matters in some fateful way. But when you grow up in dire straits, everything that happens matters because mistakes, misplays, and missed opportunities are costly. So that's how I grew up—alert. I try not to overlook anything. I don't discount anything. Hear me now: No discounts!

In my estimation, about 10 percent of all salespeople are top-tier earners, another 10 percent are chronic losers and the 80 percent in the middle do well enough, some plenty well. Some people get by at the low end of the middle group; some live large at the high end of the middle group. The annual income of the Street-Smart salesperson won't fall below the high end of the middle group—those sales reps who could double their money just by looking at themselves as professionals, updating and expanding their knowledge and skills on an ongoing basis.

If you understand the psychology as well as the procedures of the sales trade, you can sell anything. If the bottom drops out of the market for truck tires, you can move to a job selling auto parts; more daring leaps are possible. Street-Smart salespeople will always find a way to make money. Where other people make work for themselves, Street-Smart salespeople make *opportunities* for themselves.

Note that the option to make more money by putting in more effort and time is an option available only to salespeople and entrepreneurs, not to salaried workers. If you think a job in law or education would be less financially risky over the course of a working life than sales, I have to say I disagree. I have interviewed many underemployed lawyers, disaffected college professors, and other disgruntled professionals, some still carrying a balance due on their education. Shell-shocked by their failure to foresee or build a sufficient nest egg in such time-honored professions, they often tell me they always thought they'd be good at sales, but always regarded sales as too uncertain an enterprise to take seriously.

To my survival-based way of thinking, if you think you have the skills to succeed at selling, it's too risky *not* to try! I mean it. Good salespeople can do well even in the most challenging times.

In my experience, when sales people anywhere in the middle 80 percent fail to meet a target, they point a finger at other people and situations conveniently beyond their control. The worst of them consistently blame bad timing, bad luck, miscommunication, someone else's stealth or stupidity. They have a whole litany of excuses to draw upon. This is their *modus operandi*.

By contrast, when high-performance salespeople (those in or near the top 10 percent) fail to hit a target, they take a good long look at themselves and their game plan—the parts of the selling scenario they *can* control. An aversion to failure is what drives people like me to constantly refine our *modus operandi*. I got mine the hard way.

Poor people, you may be surprised to hear, can be highly creative, productive, and self-motivated individuals. They have at least one mountain to climb every day and, in most cases, several more. They're unemployed or working two or three jobs, with mouths to feed, maybe someone sick or elderly to care for. In my experience, the creativity and ambition of a poor person develops in direct proportion to his comprehension that he—or she—is on their own in this world, with nothing and no one to fall back on. In the professional world, this is called *accountability*.

Still, the efforts of the very poor generally pay no more dividend than survival. Assuming as I always have, however, that failure is not an option, my professional focus has been so intense from the get-go that every time I looked up, no matter what product I was selling, I was a top earner. And my lifelong attention to my professional development continues to pay off.

Unlike too many salespeople, I regard myself as a professional in the very same way a doctor or a lawyer does. To be a professional requires considerable investment of time and resources over the course of a career in order to keep pace with developments and opportunities, establish and expand industry associations, build and enhance your skill set. A professional does not report to a desk and perform management-assigned tasks. A professional cultivates an ever-expanding community of customers and colleagues and fine-tunes a specialized repertoire of social and practical skills in support of a self-generated plan.

One of the best things that can come to an ambitious professional is a mentor, especially at the start of a career. For argument's sake, let's say a mentor is literally a "wise guy," someone with knowledge and connections you don't possess. Where I come from, a person looked kindly upon by a wiseguy was home free! And you don't actually have to pursue a mentor, (though in one important instance I did) you just have to earn the notice of someone in a position of authority who can help you advance, advise you on strategies and decisions.

About 25 years ago, I heard a fellow named Bill Sardi speak at a sales training session. We were both working for the same company. I was so impressed with and intrigued by what he had to say that I made it my business to bring myself to his attention. Over the next few years, Bill introduced me to many important concepts, chiefly to the understanding that the individual features of a product are the least important variables in a sales equation. In order to build a long-term, highly rewarding sales relationship, he said, it is far more important for the seller to get inside a customer's head, to understand what he is up against, where he is professionally and where he wants to go. Once you understand his stresses and aspirations, he advised, "Your product becomes your currency." A product's particular bells and whistles are much more attractive and appreciated when they are introduced as a solution to a customer-specific problem, not just the latest thing. I'll always be grateful to him for this insight.

I found another mentor very early on by the name of Marty Ehrlich. Marty passed away some years ago, but previously I had spoken with him regularly long after we had stopped working for the same company. By the time I met Marty, he wasn't the hungriest salesman I'd ever known, not by a long shot. He made a good living selling pharmaceuticals and had no interest in working any harder than he already did. Instead, he put in extra time to encourage me because he saw something in me that reminded him of his younger, hungrier self. I was flattered by his attention, of course, and his belief in me helped me believe too. He lit a fire in me that is still burning.

Marty was a smooth-talking New Yorker with no college degree but a world of street smarts. Among many insights and lessons he imparted to me was his instruction to always use first names in all professional dealings. He reinforced this point by getting all the gals working in the nearby MacDonald's to greet me by my name whenever I came in. Point made. Never once did I not enjoy the good feeling I got from those first-name hellos.

The most important thing Marty preached was that selling is a profession, not an avocation. He lamented that "99 percent" of salespeople never invest a single dime in their professional development. "They don't ask questions, they don't read books, don't attend seminars, don't do their research. *That's* your opening," he'd say. "Be smarter than the other guy. You don't have to know all about everything; you just have to know enough to distinguish yourself from the rest of the herd." Remember his words!

In Marty's—and now my own—experience, sales-people who fail to thrive share one huge, and very solvable problem: They want to be loved by their customers. And because customers generally have a poor and deeply embedded opinion of salespeople, sales reps tend to share this overall dim view of their occupation. After all, they were raised in the same culture. The Street-Smart salesperson, however, uses a customer's assumed distaste for him and all he represents to upend that customer's expectations as a first step in establishing a long-term, mutually rewarding business relationship based on the "fact" that the Street-Smart rep is one in a million. Simple math.

As a kid, I could never afford to care what people thought of me. There is no crying in baseball. Forget what anyone thinks about the anxious life of a salesperson, and never succumb to such demeaning assumptions. Instead, aspire to personal uniqueness and unemotional professionalism. You will reap the rewards. It's to your advantage that no one takes you seriously. As you'll come to see, their disdain actually gives you room to operate.

■ ■ ■

Rarely is a single aspect of a sales transaction improved by there being some bond of affection between buyer and seller. In fact, just the opposite is true: Personal affections muddy the waters of a business relationship. After all, what's a fair price between friends?

The Street-Smart salesperson knows better than to risk commingling the social and the professional. In nearly 30 years of selling, I can still count on one hand the number of customers who have ever thought to ask me, all on their own, "Anthony, how're you doing? How's your health, your family?" That's fine with me because it tells me that my customers and I understand each other; we know we're all about business. None of my real friendships are so one-sided. My conversations with customers are congenial and completely focused on the matter at hand. We don't work toward friendship; we work toward *trust* instead. It's less complicated and more rewarding that way. In business, as in life, trust is a much more stable commodity than camaraderie, and it is the strongest possible foundation for a long-term professional relationship.

Customers want what they perceive to be the best deal and they want to *use* the salesperson—you—to get it. Never forget that. Why would you want to be friends with someone who only wants to use you? You don't, and if you do, you shouldn't. You want the customer's *business* and her confidence in your ability to deliver, not her friendship.

Success at what's called "inside sales"—the kind we associate with department and shoe stores—hinges on real or pretend empathy or shallow, trend-deep appearances. Such pretenses are the enemy of success in "outside" sales, the kind of sales that have made me rich, the sale of supplies to business. That is to say, drinking glasses to restaurants, heavy equipment to building contractors, pianos to pianists, whatever. In business-to-business transactions, the salesperson gets a cut and takes home a percentage of the money. That's a huge, defining difference. Just about anyone can get a job in inside sales as long as he looks presentable and doesn't have a rap sheet. But you've probably noticed that there are few career sales clerks. A department store clerk may sometimes collect a commission, but her income is constrained by who happens to walk onto the floor; she can't generate her own business. Inside salespeople are order takers; outside salespeople are order *getters*. Street-Smart salespeople are order *creators*.

It's unfortunate, but people who have worked inside sales rarely try their hand at sales of goods and services. That's because when they worked in "sales" they had to put up with all kinds of nonsense from management and customers alike, up to and including belligerence and theft. They hated the hours, the gossiping, the coffee, the uniform. Complaints will vary. But about the last thing a person wants to do after leaving a dead-end inside sales job is get into outside sales. And that's a pity, because outside sales is where the nonsense isn't—and the money *is*. Lots of it.

Working outside sales compares best to being an entrepreneur and running your own company. Entrepreneurs are often celebrated as visionaries, but any of them will tell you that brainstorming is only part, maybe even the smallest part, of their achievement and sustained success. The willingness to take risks has a lot more to do with their achievement. A salesperson (we'll abandon the "outside" distinction from here on), like any entrepreneur, is in charge of identifying prospects and negotiating sales, marketing, public relations, billing, accounting, reporting, you name it. What the job doesn't require is employee management beyond self-discipline. Nevertheless, the success of any sales or entrepreneurial venture will correspond directly to personal initiative and determination—often called self-discipline.

To become a high-performance salesperson, everything you do during the workday must have a single purpose: to grow your business. If you can't connect your actions to a direct benefit to your business, you are either wasting time on ill-considered activities or working without a *quid pro quo*—the fair exchange of one service for another. These and other bad habits can and must be unlearned to your benefit and long-term reward. Starting now.

The Street-Smart Seven!

- A customer's disdain for salespeople is what gives you room to operate. It's your job to give him reasons to take you seriously!

- Always aspire to uniqueness. Set yourself apart.

- Too few salespeople take their potential seriously enough to become authorities in their field. Don't be one of them. Fine-tune your selling skills: read, attend seminars, and participate in professional organizations.

- Find a mentor, or be one. Either way, you win.

- Every hour of your workday has one purpose only: to advance the cause of making you money.

(continued)

(continued)

- Fail to close a deal? Look inward. Don't blame other people or circumstances.
- No discounts! Don't discount observations without good reason. Be alert, analytical. Take notes and consult them.

II

Street-Smart Selling

CHAPTER
5

Game-Changers

The beauty of it all is that you own it all.

—Anthony Belli

I've never met a high-performance salesperson who didn't feel that he or she was entirely responsible for their success. I certainly take full credit for mine. High-performance reps like me "own"—that is, take responsibility for—the tenor and progress of every selling cycle and every outcome. We are the most skillful practitioners of the justly famous Oz Principle of Leadership Accountability®, which holds that success is attained through "a personal choice to rise above one's circumstances and demonstrate the necessary ownership to achieve a desired result."[1] That is a most high-minded and highly regarded way to say what I learned on my way up: That to rise above your circumstances, you must first assess the obstacles, and then, *in a way particular to you*, hatch and carry through plans to surmount them.

Obviously, assessing comes first. Sometimes an obstacle is a hindrance, other times an excuse-provider, at still other times a leveraging device. I try to identify any self-made obstacles first, on the assumption that I can find a way to turn that negative into a positive. Then I look at the situation objectively. How can I turn the fact that my customer disliked the last rep from my company into an opportunity without throwing the former rep under the bus? I've found, as you will, that *disarming* approaches can be very rewarding. Everyone can be touched in a positive way. Find it! The baddest guys in my neighborhood used to melt with one look at my mother.

There was a boxing gym at the junior high school at 120th Street and First Avenue. After my baseball workouts I would find a corner, jump rope, and watch the fighters. On one occasion, a fighter—older, stronger, and more skillful than the others—began to expand his workout space to include my territory, to squeeze me out as if I didn't exist. I had to make a stand or get out of there. If I said the wrong thing, I would either be decked or be made out a patsy. I approached him, removed my cap, looked him in the eye, and said, "How the f_____ . . ." (long pause here) " . . . did you learn to hit the bag that hard? I've only seen fighters on TV before, but watching you is amazing. I can't even focus on my jump rope!" As I transitioned from nuisance to fan, I got back my real estate.

The point is that it is possible to neutralize most enemies, meaning that if you're flexible and creative enough, it is also possible to convert customers into fans. Are you? Anytime you're considering your next move, you need to discern when to play the underdog and when to be the aggressor. Because they have made steady money while drinking the Kool-Aid of conventional sales wisdom, the vast majority of veteran reps think they know all the possible angles and pitfalls of the selling game, all the tried-and-true opens and closes, and so on. They don't. They can't. The possibilities are too many. I can hear the words of another sales mentor, Les Gottlieb, in my ear: "There's no such thing as hard sell or soft sell. There's only dumb sell and smart sell."

If they're going to put in some extra effort, they'll typically do no more than plan to get out of bed earlier. They won't go to a seminar and try out the new tactics they learned. They'll just put in a longer day doing the same old. I'm amazed at the way people congratulate themselves for getting up early in the morning. Everybody who's serious about *anything* gets up early in the morning. Rising in the dark is a *minimum* requirement for business success. But people will boast of how early they get out of bed to make their money. Really? Big money?

Let's assume that you and all of your competition get out of bed early, make phone calls, pay visits, ply customers with free samples and demonstrations, free lunches, dinners, and tickets. How might you differentiate yourself from this worm-getting herd? Get up earlier and make two or three more calls in a day? I'd call that virtuous, but not a differentiator, and certainly not financially rewarding enough to satisfy the Street-Smart Salesman.

To my mind, the *real* differentiator, the real game-changer in sales, has much less to do with time than with skill, specifically *people* skills, what are popularly called "street smarts," to my mind the most overlooked, misunderstood, undervalued, and underutilized weapon in the contemporary sales rep's arsenal. Though conventional wisdom holds that the qualities that set someone or something apart are key to success in selling, somehow these vaunted differentiators supposedly are limited to *product* quality and performance, to deal structures and other defined quantities. Notably absent from the list of desirable differentiators is the concept of anything being different about the sales*person*. As far as I know, no one has ever quantified the value of a salesperson who sets himself apart from all the others a customer has known—*in terms of his demeanor*.

This industry-wide failure to quantify the value of personal differentiation is, to me, a shocking oversight that's good for one thing only: a long-term visa for the Land of Missed Opportunities. To me, it's absolutely nonsensical. Buying and selling takes place between individuals, doesn't it? And individuals have likes and dislikes, habits, foibles, passions, fears, talents, anxieties, and more, so much more. Yet, conventional wisdom calls for all sales reps to dress and behave with little variation and, furthermore, to treat all buyers alike, without any regard for personality, experience, motivation, or any other *customer-specific* factor. As you read about how I approach the game of selling, I want you to keep in mind at all times that selling transactions are person-to-person, ultimately face-to-face, encounters. The better you are able to influence the behavior of your customer based on your understanding of his personal psychology, the richer you will both become.

Salespeople operate on the outermost ring of their companies' managerial sphere (a position that is exacerbated if the salesperson is a telecommuter), and the one closest to the public. Now, the general public is full of all kinds of people, isn't it? Would you ever consider approaching all people with the same message in the same way? Why do salespeople do it? Because conventional wisdom tells them to do it and they never think to ask, much less address or answer my obvious question.

To boot, a salesperson's performance affects his company's bottom line and the careers of some or many or all of its employees. Therefore, a salesperson's stats are constantly reviewed with the scrutiny that Yankee coaches bring to day-to-day management. And while salespeople are answerable to management, they are also answerable to their clients and, by extension, to the companies their clients work for, some of which may embrace policies and standards incompatible with their own. Given the countless variables at play in any human-to-human encounter, a salesperson must, I insist, be adaptive and creative with each customer in order to thrive. Let the customer be a differentiator! Yet the majority of sales trainers, even sales gurus, preach time-honored selling scenarios, not people skills and personal reliance.

Why do the salesforces of the world need to embrace the methods of the Street-Smart Salesman? It's because *all* customers are egocentric. Completely. They may not be egotists personally, but the buyer-seller dance casts them in a self-interested stance they have no desire to escape. However sophisticated, naive, heavy-handed, rich, poor, even dumb he is, every customer has strategies that are intended to elicit from you, at a bare minimum, free advice or the lowest price. All customers have *personalities* that affect their buying strategies, and Street-Smart sellers figure out how to exploit them to mutual benefit.

If a salesperson doesn't come armed with professional strategies that take a customer's unique combination of personality and self-centeredness into account, he will be forever at the mercy of the script and the buyer. To be at the mercy of the buyer does not necessarily mean "No Sale," of course, just that the seller won't be making as much money as possible. This is the current state of the sales trade, in my view. It's all script and memorization, market research and product evaluations, pretend friendships and fawning relationships, free samples and follow-up calls. There's no creativity, no customization, no skill. We customize products as a way of raising

the price. Why don't we customize our client relationships as a way of raking in higher commissions? I find
it baffling.

The outside sales customer is a professional buyer.
She understands full well that salespeople want her
money. She is not disappointed in you because you're
all about money. You both are. As far as she's concerned
(and her opinions are likely supported by experience),
she's holding all the candy (schoolyard coinage), and all
you have is the hope she'll share some with you. All professional buyers have worked this playground angle to their
advantage many times over. They have convinced many a
sales rep to donate, in my opinion, scandalous amounts of
energy, assets, and expertise in the hope of doing further
business. But you can't live on hope for long.

The rock bottom reason your customer believes
you are not telling the whole truth about anything is
because she isn't. Until you give a customer a reason to
believe otherwise, she has no reason to think you're any
different from any other rep, with their rote deliveries
and management-approved offers. So ask yourself: Why
would I put my profit margin in the hands of someone
who is out to get something for nothing and doesn't trust
me? Good question, right? Yet salespeople do it every
day and all career-long.

Even if the seller is not, the buying professional is
highly aware of the value of a salesperson's experience,
generally to an extent far greater than the rep appreciates.
A customer doesn't want to pay one dollar more than

she absolutely must to benefit from a rep's professional experience, however. The seller's job, your job, is to get that customer to pay more than she planned while still feeling she got the best deal possible. How do you manage this? I'll tell you how I do it: by bringing so much value I turn the customer into my *fan*. Now, nobody was ever a fan of a guy who was just like everybody else. No, to be worthy of fans in any arena, you have to set yourself apart from your competitors. You have to bring something new to the game. What we salesmen call a differentiator ball players call a *game-changer*.

The vast majority of sales reps kick off a sales cycle by immediately succumbing to the customer's desire for free advice and product samples. I have never understood this, not from my first day at MetLife. Whenever a poor kid like me got his hands on something anybody else would want—candy, cigarettes, information—that commodity was never traded away for anything as insubstantial as hope. A nickel to hear what the pretty girl said about you: okay. A stick of gum for a (specific) baseball card: okay. But a nickel for the *promise* of payback? No way. I learned pretty fast that any kid in Jefferson Park clever enough to persuade me to part with a coin was in no hurry to pay me back. Give someone a free ride and he takes you for a chump forevermore. In fact, he's already thinking about what else he can get out of you for nothing.

Hear me now: Giving product away up front sets a bad precedent in a sales cycle. Why would a customer pay you to conduct a staff seminar when he can pump you for free advice, then address the staff himself, looking like a sage into the bargain? I never, ever do it. The net result of such behavior is always the same: The client gains valuable information and services while the sales rep, based on his ill-conceived gesture of goodwill, only gets his hopes up. I use the term "ill-conceived" because I try not to say "stupid" anymore, but the inescapable fact is that a prospect is very often satisfied with his current vendor and has no intention whatsoever of switching over to you. What he or she is most likely to want out of your meeting is to come away with free inside information and discount offers she can use to secure better terms from the rep she's been buying from for years. That's really what you're up against when you approach a prospect. What has the potential to be the game-changer, the differentiator, in such situations? Anything that upends that customer's expectations.

Customers are alike in broad ways, sure, but inside every professional buyer is a living, breathing, thinking person with opinions, habits, quotas, aspirations, trepidations, and more, all of which provide promising, and far too often unexplored, angles for a sales rep to work. In such details lies the Street-Smart seller's power!

Conventional selling systems don't encourage salespeople to delve into any of this kind of personal stuff. Personal stuff is considered a minefield. Therefore, trainers typically counsel salespeople to *monopolize* their conversations with a customer by parroting one or another company-generated script and giving that customer as little room to talk—and maybe change his mind—as possible.

Even crazier, conventional wisdom holds that customers make buying decisions based on *logic*, the assumption that they'll most likely sign on the dotted line when presented with incontrovertible evidence of product superiority or cost-effectiveness. Kill this notion. The clients of Street-Smart sellers are happy to sign their contracts because they have contributed ideas and suggestions to a process that resulted in a financial arrangement they recognize in print.

I don't dispute that logic can be a strong motivator in sales, but it's too low a common denominator for someone like me with the intention to make big money. I believe that 95 percent of all buying decisions are emotional decisions, and experience has proven to me that emotional buying decisions command higher prices. Understanding what a particular customer likes, dislikes, feels, knows, fears—these are the factors that allow the Street-Smart seller to focus on solving a customer's problems and help him express his satisfaction by paying premium prices.

Recitation of the company script will never get you to the promised land of premium prices, I promise you that. Where I come from, and wherever you come from, the motormouth is a person to be avoided whenever possible. Nobody wanted to be in the room with my poor upstairs neighbor, Ron, to listen to him counting backwards from one hundred throughout the waking hours. The collective desire to avoid him combined with his presence in my kitchen to keep hardened thieves from our door: *That's how eager we all are to avoid the motormouth.* Who wants to be subjected to warmed-over speeches that fail to acknowledge anything specific to the listener? Are you kidding? Is it any wonder your customers seem so determined to get you out of their offices as soon as possible? At least part of the reason for their impatience and disdain is that you never shut up. The other part is that they've heard it all before.

One hundred percent contrary to other sales "systems," Street-Smart selling calls for the sales representative to *say as little as possible* when engaged with a customer. By keeping quiet and *appearing to cede control* of the conversation, the Street-Smart Salesman provides himself a more wide-angle perspective through which to gain free, useful information that will enable him to conceive and deliver a dream deal for this particular client. A dream deal, in Street-Smart vocabulary, is one that treats a customer's *pain*.

Henceforth, I want *you* to perform the information extraction at the start of a sales cycle. I want you to relax, ask well-formed questions, and listen closely to the responses until you understand as much as possible about an individual customer's professional wants, needs, preferences, motivations, conflicts, and so on. The customer will appreciate and reward your attention; I guarantee it.

The information you seek is a lot like the information that allows a theater director to contrive a performance to elicit a desired response from an audience. To paraphrase the sales guru David Sandler, selling is like a Broadway show directed by a psychiatrist.[2] Salespeople are not required to be shrinks, to be sure, but the best of us practice psychology all day, every day, and, like a theater director, orchestrate the proceedings by shaping a customer's understanding of the stakes. Among the many useful skills a good stage director has is an understanding of where the metaphorical spotlight properly belongs. A Street-Smart seller understands that the spotlight should always be on the customer; that the seller is not the star of the show, no matter how elated he may be offstage. The seller is not the star, he is only the director—that is, the person of vision in control of the script and the outcome.

In East Harlem I learned that if the underdog is to have any power in a tough situation he has to influence the game by his own interpretation of the rules. I'm not talking about the laws of physics, you understand. I'm talking about the human dynamics of a situation. Most people study their way to a high school diploma, for instance; I cajoled mine. The key is to be fully present with a will to win, not just an arsenal of scripts and samples.

Let me quote the poker professional, Anthony Holden: "No poker player ever earned any respect simply by pulling good cards; the best players are those who can turn indifferent hands into winners through psychological mastery of their opponents."[3] That says it all, but to live it, you have to believe it. And to believe it, you have to try it—my way. The best players are always alert, always calculating, and always ready to bust a move.

And you know why? Because as David Mamet, serious poker player and screenwriter of *Glengarry Glen Ross*, put it, "Opportunity may knock, but it seldom nags."[4]

Anybody can play a good hand, then. Learning to win with bad cards is the key to winning at poker *and* selling—and it requires *bluffing*. Bluffing is the high art of poker and the real thrill of the game. By skillfully pretending to hold a strong hand, you can drive all the other players out of the hand without ever having to show your cards. Successful poker players don't blame their losses on lousy cards or their opponents' dumb luck because they are professionals, not gamblers. Gamblers make bad bets based on reasons as insubstantial as hunches and superstition. Professionals understand that poker is, as much as any game, like life, full of rules made to be bent, broken, and ignored in combination with unchanging probabilities. Professional players know that you can't bend the rules effectively unless you have absorbed all the mathematical probabilities, and the best of them can take the game all the way to a double bluff, losing with a good hand to create a false impression of their skill level in order to bring home a huge pot on another deal.

Weak players get caught bluffing because they know they don't know the math and are (rightly) too scared to bluff enough to get good at it. It takes nerve (and in poker, money) to practice bluffing, especially since bluffing or any other tactic works best if you employ it in a situation where it's least expected. However, bluffing for its own sake is buffoonery or, worse, gambling. The

Street-Smart don't count cards; we understand the psychology of pain and the appeal of pain relief. We don't bluff; we orchestrate!

Remember: It is to your advantage that no one takes salespeople seriously. The seller's ability to analyze and act upon close observations of a customer's behavior constitutes the relatively unchanging probabilities of the selling game. The Street-Smart seller's edge is founded upon his or her confidence and self-reliance.

A selling cycle is hardly the World Series of Poker, with a wily veteran in every chair, however. Chances are a buyer is nowhere near the player a Street-Smart seller is. If you've been afraid that you'll get nowhere with a prospect if you don't fork over some free samples on the first date, try withholding the candy a few times and watch what happens. You'll find that customers are almost helplessly intrigued to know what it is you're holding that you're so reluctant to give away. Really. Why? *Because no one else does it.* You see, while the Street-Smart seller labors in the same fields as his competition, he or she has *a game plan that's new to the customer*, one in which the differentiator is the *seller*, not the product or the price or anything else. Just *you*.

Never solve a customer's problems too quickly! *Never* make what you do look easy. To do so only diminishes the value of your time and expertise and, in the end, makes you look weak. Fold a two-pair hand too soon and you will grieve over the one pair that won. Even if you know exactly what your next move will be, let the customer know how helpful your conversation has been, and get going. I mean it. *Always* let time pass before you present the solution to his pain. What the fortunate customers of Street-Smart sellers experience is a breath of fresh air in the welcome form of a sales representative curiously unlike the others they've dealt with, one able to deliver more customized value than they've ever experienced. Street-Smart sellers make a buyer look like a genius to company management, too. The way we play, everybody wins. Without lowering—indeed, by steadily raising the stakes as a poker player would—we find ways to boost the buyer's professional standing in tandem with our own.

Raising the stakes is an art in itself, to be sure. Don't be too quick about that either! Things that happen too fast are not trustworthy and breed suspicion. If you say to me, I'm thinking of selling my car for five thousand dollars and I say I'll give you five thousand dollars right now, you don't think, lucky me, I've sold my car for five thousand dollars! No, you think maybe I should have asked for six, or seven, or eight thousand. Because getting five was too easy.

Let there be no hubris on the seller's part! Talk with your client about his problems, and get him to put a figure to what a solution would be worth to his business. *Always find out what a solution is worth to a customer before you attach a price to it.* Let's say a client estimates that a solution to a particular problem could bring in another quarter of a million dollars in added business over the next few years. Now, when the client asks what you think the solution would cost, you can say it's probably going to be expensive. How expensive, he wants to know. Well, once a customer has put a price tag on the solution (in this case, $250,000), you can price your solution at a premium because your efforts come with a stated dollar value attached.

My assertion is that the seller can control a buyer's behavior without the immediate support of any market-researched freebies, bells or whistles, contrary to any sales training system I've ever come across. I am living proof that it can be done, and I bet you can do it, too. If you are in an industry that relies on freebies—and many salespeople are—then you must make your freebies somehow special, pegged to the customer's good behavior, to measures of time, quantity, and so on. Give a freebie value or don't give it at all, because while value can't always be measured in dollars and cents, it always provides a psychological benefit.

The Street-Smart seller you can become is a relaxed, good listener who asks only nonthreatening questions and *leaves the sales aids in the trunk of the car.* You heard me. Would you dare to show up for a first sales meeting with nothing but your wits about you? That's what I'm telling you to do. Of course, once you've seen how well my approach can pay off, you won't regard your reluctance to distribute freebies to a new customer as a bluff of any kind, but as your *m.o.*, your Street-Smart style.

It takes a lot of sophistication to get people to give their money to you, no doubt about it. As I've said, the first thing a prospect does is lie to the salesman. Think about it. How often do you tell a sales clerk that you're "just looking?" All the time, you say? You lie because, like everybody else, you worry that the sales clerk is somehow, as if by black magic, going to make you buy something you don't need and can't afford. A high-performance salesperson attempts to resist selling a customer anything he doesn't need or can't afford. A high-performance salesperson solves his customers' problems, and by steadily relieving the customers' fears, he never becomes one of them. As you make the transition from peddler to professional problem-solver, you will begin to earn a customer's trust, and learn how with trust comes increasing control of the sales cycle. The customer who trusts you, you see, looks forward to your call. Reverse the conventional wisdom. Make yourself this differential chart for you to consult whenever you're thinking about your next move. Make it wallet size!

Seven Qualities of the Street-Smart Salesman

- Relax! Be casual.
- Don't be a robot and just follow the program. Be creative: You are a stage director—the person of vision in control of the script and the outcome!

(continued)

(continued)

- Don't make presentations. Be a detective beginning an investigation.

- Don't be a proctologist, be a psychiatrist. Let the customer talk while you listen and make notes. Let your few words prove that you've been listening.

- Don't be in a hurry. Things that happen too fast cannot be trusted. Let time pass between offers and customers will look forward to your calls.

- Don't believe that, in the end, the product closes the sale. Not even close! Anything in the universe can close a sale.

- You can win with any hand you are dealt. Your brain supplies the magic.

A Street-Smart Super Seven!

- Have a style and a game plan that's new to the customer. Understand the value of a game-changer, of giving your clients reasons to see you as a breed apart.

- Never kick off a sales cycle with freebies. If you must, give freebies value by pegging them to good customer behavior.

- Your customers appreciate the value of your experience, even if you don't. Always put a price on it!

- The buyer's emotions are the prime motivator in sales, not logic. Try withholding the candy and watch what happens.

- Never solve a customer's problems too quickly! Don't ever make solutions look easy. Find out what a solution to a particular problem is worth to a customer's business before putting a price on it.

- Leave the sales aids in the car for the first *two* meetings with a prospect. Let there be no doubt you didn't forget them the first time, instead that you don't *need* them.

- Resist selling a customer anything he doesn't need or can't afford, unless he demands it.

6

Shut Up!

They talk when they should listen.
—Don Corleone, *The Godfather*

How many times have you heard someone complain, or complained yourself, that someone wouldn't shut up and let anybody else talk? We tend to characterize marathon talkers—motormouths—as having an oversized need for control. That's a fair assessment, and control of a conversation is for sure a very powerful means of getting one's way, if only in the short term. Customers feel the same way. Given that your customer also seeks to control the sales conversation and is only willing to reveal as much as he thinks it useful for you to know, how do you turn the conversational tables to your advantage? Upend them!

Most sales training systems teach that for the salesperson to gain and maintain control of the sales cycle, the seller must seize control of the conversation right out of the gate and keep talking all the way through to the signature on the contract. Supposedly, keeping the customer from getting a word in edgewise is the best way to keep him from scuttling the deal the seller has in mind. I'm sorry, but there's a reason that the wire-to-wire strategy is among the least-used in horse racing: because it demands constant superior performance from beginning to end. Sure, the wire-to-wire gambit can work every so often, but no thoroughbred trainer worth his oats would make it a habit. And a racing oval is a far less complicated path to negotiate than a sales cycle.

Yet this monopolizing chatter is the industry-approved *m.o.* for the sales professional, despite the fact that it flies in the face of research revealing that good *listening* skills are the best predictors of success in sales![1] Clearly, this industry-wide behavior wouldn't persist if it wasn't generally supportive of company bottom lines; not all salespeople, after all, are able to appreciate and negotiate the nuances of human behavior, their own or their customers', in order to adopt the loose-limbed approach I recommend. Every salesperson would experience some improvement, though: A blind pig scores a truffle now and again because blindness doesn't affect the task's more important sense of smell. I preach that the most important sense in sales is *listening*.

In my old neighborhood, every kid seemed to have a black-clad grandmother who never spoke and claimed not to understand a word of English, yet seemed to know the personal business of the entire English-speaking world in lurid detail. People will say all sorts of things out loud in front of people they think don't understand what's being said. Silence can be *very* empowering. Therefore, the Street-Smart salesperson is skilled in the twin listening arts of Italian East Harlem: remaining silent and playing dumb.

When I advocate that you "play dumb," I don't mean that I want you to affect stupidity, but rather to be genuinely humble, quiet and curious about your customer. Because people will also tell all sorts of things to someone they think is listening and paying attention, precisely the kind of free, exploitable information my mentor Marty Ehrlich was so skillful at eliciting. You'll be amazed how much mileage you can get out of a simple, "I don't understand. Can you explain that a little further?" Your customer will find your curiosity flattering, refreshing and then probably unwittingly reveal something useful about himself and/or his situation, something you couldn't have known if you'd been doing all the talking. How's that for a new start?

Nothing gets a person to reveal himself more quickly and effectively than a whiff of dead air followed by a considerate question that proves you've been listening.

It's true in life and it's true in sales. I want your customer to be surprised and a little delighted to find himself, not just his budget, as a focus of your attention. *A* focus, you understand, not *the* focus. Your relationship is about business and establishing trust, not one thing more. You don't want to be his pal; you want to be his savior.

Never interrupt a customer while she's talking. Pay attention to what she's saying and look her in the eye the whole time. Wait your turn to speak and when it comes, pick up the customer's conversational thread. Never change the subject abruptly or you will alienate your customer to some costly degree. Ask yourself: How do you feel when you're talking about something important to you and the next sentence out of your listener's mouth reflects no knowledge of what you just said? Are you likely to reward that person for such behavior? No. The Street-Smart seller shifts conversational direction with a customer *only* to lead the dialogue back to business (from, say, talk of his children's scholastic achievements). But so long as business is his topic, we're all ears. What we learn helps us on our journey toward the promised land of premium prices.

Never expend energy guessing what your customer is going to say next, either. Be present in the moment, listening. Analyze as you go, make good mental notes. The information you are collecting will enable you to make a *Godfather*-ly offer that cannot be refused. After a meeting, write down your "read" on this customer, her personality, style, circumstances, what motivates her to buy. Consult these notes before each subsequent discussion with this customer; do not rely on memory entirely. Small details can translate into big payouts, believe me, and other profitable insights and patterns will emerge over time.

As I've said, it's no accident that in all my years as a salesman, I've never had a customer try to figure out what makes *me* happy. My customer doesn't care about me personally. It's not in his best interest to care. Your customer doesn't care about you either. I want you to factor this universal truth into all your business conversations from this day forward because *the customer's allegiance to himself is precisely what empowers the Street-Smart seller.* We let the customer do the bulk of the talking because we are in the business of eliciting exploitable information that allows us to create value.

■ ■ ■

Curiously, even as conventional selling systems preach that a non-stop verbal barrage is crucial to getting a customer to "Yes," they also insist that cultivating a personal bond with a customer over time is the only way to create the atmosphere of trust needed to sustain a loyal relationship. I have at least two problems with this way of thinking.

First of all, it takes too long—weeks, even months— to build any kind of rapport, no matter how phony. A few pressure-free visits (nothing to sign!), plus the free pens and key chains, a lunch, a dinner, or both, or several; maybe a ballgame, some tickets. No matter how much time and money you devote to building some bogus camaraderie with a client, in the end, you will be taken advantage of by a now-insatiable customer who will always and forever regard you as a borderline-desperate salesperson keen to do his bidding. Such coddled customers will string you along with the confidence (emphasis on the "con") of the most inveterate gold-digger, telling half-truths for as long as the relationship lasts and extracting all manner of treasure in the process. In fact, you may be assured that such a customer is feasting on your competitor's dime, too.

Maybe you think I'm painting an unduly unflattering picture of customers. I'm not! *All* buyers are egocentric. When I'm buying, I'm self-serving too. Who isn't? I might say I have less money or time to spend than I really do, for instance; there are any number of ways to duck out of a sale. What the Street-Smart seller does is *disarm* the customer so that his usual strategies don't seem to apply to our relationship—*because you're not like other sales reps*. In fact, Street-Smart selling requires that *customers become as curious about me as I am about them*—and as quickly as possible. I ensure this by defying all their experience and expectations.

Again, the dyed-in-the-wool techniques work well enough that the entire multibillion-dollar sales training industry is based on them, but those techniques and profit margins are not enough for the Street-Smart likes of you and me. The conventional approaches don't encourage—in fact, they actually discourage—any creativity, any improvisation, on the part of the salesperson. And on top of that, they foster a festering anxiety in armies of sales reps completely dependent upon the same scripts for subtly different circumstances. Invariably, salespeople come to dread the exercise, the semi-frenzied robotic performance anxiety that comes with trying to keep something awful from happening—in this case, from coming away empty-handed. Buyers dread it too: Who wants to watch someone struggle? As time goes by, this mounting anxiety causes too many a sales career to stall. A salesperson can only play the unwelcome visitor so many times a day so many years. After that, it's too demoralizing. Who wants to spend 40 years in sales pushing a hard sell and trying to keep their customers from getting a word in edgewise? I sure don't. I'm trying to have a little fun every day.

For the long term, believe me, once you have demonstrated an ability to listen to a customer's issues, then conceive and deliver on a deal that will address, even solve, one or more of his problems, that customer will stick with you, even become your champion. The best news is that it doesn't have to take months or years to establish this kind of mutually remunerative relationship; it can be born of the first face-to-face meeting, if you're a good enough information extractor. Once you've provided superior value, helped him look good to his superiors, you're of more value to him than he is to you. Quite a reversal, no? Who's the candyman now?

And guess what? Unlike the anxious salesperson, *the customer doesn't mind being the pushy one*, doesn't mind it one bit. He likes to think he's in charge. This is another human quality the conventional methodology fails to incorporate. Why *should* the customer mind being cast in this role? The time he spends dealing with you is only a few minutes, certainly not long enough for him to question whether he was meant for this line of work, as so often happens with salespeople. And as far as my pusher-customer knows, he's in charge of the subject and direction of our conversations and always comes out ahead when he deals with me instead of the other guy.

So I say let the customer lead; better him than you. He gets a thrill and you get top dollar. That's what I call Street-Smart.

■   ■   ■

The Cure for What Ails

On a cold call to a Manhattan client, I quickly uncovered the source of his professional pain. He wasn't exactly fresh out of school but he was still very ambitious, married with children and, it turned out, fearful that his business could not generate sufficient volume to build the empire he had in mind. I listened a lot and exploited my understanding of his fear just a little, but to both our lasting benefit. "I know it would be awful if no one walked through those doors," I said, giving voice to what I'd understood him to say. Now that he could tell I'd been listening—he hadn't used those exact words, so he knew I was summarizing—I could be sure he'd listen to me. I let him know that I was a top earner in my field and outlined a package deal I'd put together to help someone else build a thriving business. The next sentence out of his mouth was, "Do you think you could help me?"

"Perhaps," I said.

Perhaps? Perhaps! Not what he was (or you were) expecting, right? This is where it really got interesting, because it just so happened that I was *so* busy at the time, my calendar *so* full, really and truly, that maybe a week or two passed before I could cycle back to this potential customer. I wasn't worried about losing him; people passionately want what they cannot have. Unable to wait a minute longer, he telephoned me. I listened again, with a secret smile. Realizing how badly this fellow wanted my attention, I called for a "time out" and put him off another week. What did he do in the interim? He called the president of my company to *demand* that I work with him. I did, of course, and he was one of my best customers for 15 years, until he sold his (very successful) business.

The Street-Smart Seven!

- Practice the twin listening arts of Italian East Harlem: remaining silent and playing dumb. Listen with genuine curiosity and don't say much, except to indicate that you're paying attention. People will reveal a lot to someone they know to be listening.

- Never expend energy guessing what your customer is going to say next.

- People—especially prospects—want what they can't have.

- Never change the subject abruptly. If talk wanders too far afield, bring it back to business by reminding the customer how busy you *both* are. Don't do anything that suggests you don't have a full calendar.

- After a meeting or phone call, write down your "read" on the customer. Consult your notes before speaking again and add to them as you go. Build that profile continuously, over months and years. Things change!

- Make your customers as curious about you as you are about them.

- Let the customer lead. He gets a thrill and you get top dollar.

7

Nothing Is As
It Appears

Not everything that can be counted counts, and not everything that counts can be counted.

—Albert Einstein

In any selling scenario, the meaning of a gesture, a statement, a smile, a slip of the tongue, may not be entirely clear in the moment. But not only is there more concealed behind such superficialities than often can be readily appreciated, what a customer reveals in unconscious ways is likely to remain true. That's why the Street-Smart Salesman lets a customer do the lion's share of the talking no matter how many years they do business together—decades even. The more a customer reveals to the seller over time, the more enhanced the seller's ability to part that customer from more of his company's money.

Some time ago, a rep on my salesforce called me to report that a 20-year customer for whom she was lately responsible had defected to the competition. As far as my rep knew and insisted, the client's decision to quit us was totally product-driven; our goods just didn't measure up, or some such technical nonsense. Out of the blue, two decades into a business relationship, this customer suddenly requires product standards our company can't meet? Was blaming the company's supposedly slipping product standards really the best way for the rep to explain to the boss why she'd lost a customer after 20 years?

I sure wasn't buying it. Over the course of 20 years, there'd been plenty of times when a competitor had one or another better product; that couldn't be the explanation. So I e-mailed the customer myself in search of the real story. I began by saying that I fully accepted his decision and that the purpose of my e-mail was not to change his mind but to help me understand the factors that drove his decision; why a 20-year relationship had been broken. True to form, I put him in apparent control of the conversation.

His almost immediate, so-glad-you-asked response took the form of a phone call. I was correct, he said, that we'd had an outstanding, mutually rewarding relationship for many years. Already, I was making progress. His opening remark told me he was upset about what had happened, and that he didn't really want to scuttle the business relationship. Then came the kicker, the exposed root of his dissatisfaction: He was angry that my company had not hired his daughter when she'd graduated from college two years before. He was quick to add that he knew I knew nothing about this—he still wanted me to like him and/or do something for his daughter—but that other people in my company knew of his wish, that loyalty is a two-way street, and so on.

So our customer had gone looking for a new vendor because he felt betrayed, not because another company had a better product, though that was the excuse he used. My rep had accepted his phony techno-babble excuse at face value because it gave her cover, but I looked at the whole of his behavior over 20 years and pursued a different line of inquiry that led to the truth. True to form, by giving him plenty of room to blow me off without another word, I came away with an instructive story I then used to school my salesforce—and now you. Talk is cheap and nothing is entirely as it appears.

If my sales rep had been talking and listening to this customer in any reality-based, people-oriented way for the previous few years, she would have known about the customer's hopes for his daughter and we'd still have our customer. But she'd been talking too much to listen to her customer's aspirations!

The point is this. As a salesperson, you should put your money, time, and effort into *people* who are worth the money, time, and effort, not into companies. Find your people. People are not always what they seem, so test even the obvious things you think are true about a person. Where I come from, sometimes the cops were the good guys and sometimes they weren't. Same for the wiseguys. So watch behaviors, observe carefully, and take notes. Peel that onion.

Case Study: How Did I Get This Customer Back?

I knew that the same passion that had driven this customer away could now bring him back into the fold if I acted quickly. I suggested we have dinner. Over a thick steak, he relived for me the feeling of being "dissed" by my company after years of solid business. I listened attentively, nodding with understanding, and said, with genuine regret, "It sounds like there's nothing I can do to fix this." I made no suggestions. A moment passed, and then, just to end the silence, he proceeded to outline for me precisely the terms under which he would consider rekindling our business relationship. We then came to a new arrangement. By appearing to cede all power to him, I unleashed his inner top dog, the dictator of terms. It is human nature to want to be able to fix things to your liking. *Give customers the opportunity to be the fixer, especially when they least expect it.* Let the customer tell you how he likes it!

The Street-Smart Seven!

- Very few things are as they appear. Peel the onion!
- You can only know when to play the lion and when to play the lamb if you are alert and *listening*.
- Words matter, but behavior matters more.
- Understand that what a customer reveals in unconscious ways is likely to remain true.
- Customers will try to blame things that are out of the seller's control to avoid being pressured.
- Give customers opportunities to be the dictator of terms. Allowing your customer to help define the business relationship will allow you to help justify premium prices.
- Never forget that selling is a *game*.

CHAPTER

8

Managing First Impressions

Is that the way you look?

— James Taylor

Indulge me for a moment. Ask yourself: Why is it important to look your best for a job interview? The answer is simple and twofold: The interviewer has limited time to assess your suitability and zero tolerance for risk. The way you look in person is easily as crucial to your getting a job as the way you look on paper or anything you say or do during your interview. Steve Jeffes, the crusading author of *Appearance Is Everything*, argues that appearance discrimination plays a little-understood role in *all* relationships[1] (business, academic, personal), and he has even argued for an amendment to the Civil Rights Act of 1964 to address it.

People who look good have an easier path in life. It's the truth, so why fight it? Why not look good instead? Your look is your brand and branding is both the most immediate and potentially long-lasting form of differentiation. The boost a guy could get from a single cool item of clothing was one of the earliest lessons I learned in East Harlem, me with the one faded pair of pants, one pair of taped-up shoes, one threadbare shirt, one dingy jacket (with a once good-looking racing stripe down the sleeves). A well-put-together person, male or female, even if not classically or anywhere near handsome or beautiful, always gets the benefit of the doubt from a stranger. Plus, when you look good, you feel good, meaning you radiate confidence. And confidence is what encourages others to give you, at minimum, a chance.

In my experience however, most salespeople, like most people, dress like amateurs. Honestly. They need haircuts, they don't polish their shoes, they wear stained ties. I rarely buy anything from a person who gives no thought to his or her appearance. Instinctively, I ask myself, "What else isn't this person thinking about?" I want to deal with someone who's on the ball.

A good suit, good shoes, stylish haircut, handsome watch, tasteful jewelry. These are the universally accepted trappings of success and the foundation of the business uniform. When executed well, the uniform gives a prospect no reason *not* to have confidence in you. It may sound shallow, but clothes play a big part in what people make of a stranger. In marketing parlance, these quick calculations are called *inferential beliefs*. In East Harlem, we used more colorful language. We would say, "If the bathroom is filthy, how clean is the kitchen?"

Very occasionally, I'll admit, I meet a high-performance salesperson who dresses like a slob. There are exceptions to every rule, but you'd be ill advised to let exceptions rule your professional life. The rumpled high-performance salesperson very likely has a certain personal magnetism to go with his worn cardigan, maybe a great reputation that precedes him. Do you? Who are you scheduled to meet with next? If you present a slovenly appearance, what are the chances you will get to a second meeting with this client? You have to bring value to the equation.

In sales parlance, probabilities are called *instrumentalities*, the salesperson's estimate of the likelihood that a specific improvement will lead to a desired result. Do you believe that an enhanced appearance will lead to an increase in sales? Not by itself, I agree, but by dressing above standards you eliminate an important first-round obstacle. That, in and of itself, compresses the sales cycle (the time it takes a seller to get to a signature on a contract), especially for a beginner. Street-Smart selling is about gaining control of probabilities one by one because, as any gambler will attest, it's not gambling if the deck is stacked in your favor.

What I saw, and what I still know, is this: The cops with the stiffest collars were the toughest. The U.S. Marine with the spit shine on his shoes got all the wannabe-noticed kids in the high school to enlist. Sharp-dressed wiseguys had a trail of women. Jehovah's Witnesses, with their suits and ties to go with their Bibles, were always treated with the utmost respect and never victimized on the street. Don't fight it; look good. I keep saying how important it is to peel the onion. Your look is the first layer of *your* onion, and it doesn't have to tell the whole truth about you!

Dressing conservatively does not mean dressing without style, you understand. Neither does dressing conservatively constitute a political statement. The way a person dresses for work does not necessarily represent who he or she is in any other context. All people, however, customers included, appreciate a salesperson's stylishness only up to the point where it makes them feel poorly dressed themselves. That's why conservative styles are the best choice for sellers; they don't offend, they just convey competence. Avoid fashion extremes: Stick with classic cuts, patterns, colors, and quality fabrics. Find a good tailor and have all your business clothes fitted; you'll look and feel much more comfortable and at ease in the field, qualities your customer will gravitate toward, consciously or unconsciously. When you consider how much it costs to buy a fast-food franchise or fund a law degree, the cost of three good suits and accessories is nothing. And with your brains and savvy you can't fail to project the confidence and accomplishment that makes a quick and favorable first impression.

Funny thing is, when I first put on a suit, I felt like an imposter, no other word. But I soon found that, in the same way a poor kid can't imagine himself sitting on a corporate Board of Directors, a well-heeled person can't imagine that someone smart and ambitious like me, in my sharp new suit, was dirt poor and scrambling a short time before. More than that, I came to understand that, even if such a person did know my history, now he wouldn't care. Satisfied customers don't care where you grew up—what they care about is what you do for them. It wasn't long, maybe two weeks, before I felt that I was born to wear a suit. I loved the way I looked and what my suit said about me. In all honesty, I couldn't get enough of that feeling. I still make it a habit to wear a suit every day, whether or not I have any face-to-face meetings on my schedule. A Street-Smart Salesman is always ready.

Along the way I developed an even more dramatic way to physically, wordlessly, demonstrate that I was not like every other salesperson: I stopped carrying a brief-case. Talk about a differentiator! Hear me now: *Do not bring a briefcase or roller cart to a first meeting.* Baggage of any kind raises a red flag with staffers, beginning with the receptionist, all of whom are programmed to lock down when anyone official-looking arrives. Even if you succeed in making it past a company's gatekeepers, your luggage will put your prospect on edge. That's because as soon as a prospect sees your case, he thinks, "Here it comes, the company literature," and checks his watch. It's much better to have him notice that you are not carrying anything. It suggests radical thinking, something new in the air.

An alert mind is a much more powerful weapon than any so-called sales aid, no matter how showy or market-tested. Humping a suitcase full of sales aids over the door-sill only announces business as usual and makes a prospect resolve to get you out of the office in record time. Showing up alert and empty-handed, however, is something new under the sun. Now you have the customer's attention too. And he's enjoying the change, breathing fresh air.

Let me say one last thing about appearance: It's not all about clothes and shoes and jewelry. It's also about language, the way you talk, what you say. It's not that you have to speak the King's English; I sure don't. I don't know a lot of fancy words and phrases. But I'm *careful* about what I say because I understand that words have power. But when are words to be believed?

Think of any profanity. That word or phrase, whatever it is, however crass, probably can be used just as effectively to establish kinship as to start a fight. It's tone that makes the difference. In East Harlem, all the most disgusting words I knew were regularly used as greetings. As street slang takes hold in the national vernacular via movies and television, popular music and talk radio, we hear such words and phrases more and more. But in East Harlem I learned that words are not as important as people think they are. Words, you see, are only significant when simultaneously validated by other forms of communication.

This is a really important point, fundamental to Street-Smart selling. Overall, I consider words to be the *least* valid form of communication; People will always say anything if they're in enough of a jam. The streets taught me to give far more weight to behavior and body language than to words. If they are in agreement, I believe a little more, enough to make the deal, but I never take any words, no matter how believable, entirely to heart. Validation also has to be continuous, because circumstances change. Hone your powers of observation and bring to bear everything you know about a client every time you deal with him.

Therefore, if a customer's words are consistent with his appearance and behavior, I proceed accordingly. If they are in conflict, or newly in conflict, I try to find the source of the disconnect. Just as a teenage girl has to weigh whether her boyfriend really means it when he says he'll love her forever, so the Street-Smart seller has to assess whether his customer is really the straight shooter he presents himself to be.

Getting to the truth is the most critical aspect of a sales cycle, and getting to the truth was a skill at which my East Harlem brethren, armed and unarmed, excelled. Everyone in my neighborhood was running some kind of con. That was a given. To come out ahead, you had to decipher the con as quickly and accurately as possible.

The first rule of dealing with a con man is to dismiss every word he says. Of course, you have to identify him first; that's the tricky part! A good con man is slick enough to be believed by most people. So separate his words from gestures: Are they in sync? Does he lower his voice? Look you in the eye? Remind you of anybody? Have you been in this situation before? Take a step back: The guy you hardly know, who says he can turn your 20 into 40 in a flash—how many people would you estimate he owes money to? My estimate would be 20 to 40.

East Harlem was full of cons, not Bernie Madoff level cons, but 5- and 10- and 20-dollar survival cons. The thing is, in a poor neighborhood, no one's situation is different enough from your own that you'd *ever* give a stranger, even a near stranger, your immediate trust. I don't think I ever made the walk back to the apartment from Patsy's with a full box of pizza without picking up somebody along the way who suddenly had to speak with my brother about a possible job down at the Sanitation Department right now. What he really wanted was to bullshit my brother over a free slice of pizza. There was no job. It's a con. There was a priest in the neighborhood who always wanted to come over and talk to me about how I could live a more Christian life. But everybody knew he was dallying with one of the nuns and I knew he had his eye on my sister. So, even though he was a fully vested Catholic priest, was he to be trusted when he said he had my spiritual future in mind? When your suspicions are strong, acknowledge them, find their source. Know what to discount—in this case, the priest's collar.

Now, as then, I make assessments about the people I'm talking to quickly and, almost always, correctly. I note how they're dressed, how they present themselves. I look at the relationship between the spoken and unspoken, factoring in body language, stance, posture, and gestures. When a person is being forthright, for instance, he or she will not be avoiding eye contact or crossing and uncrossing his legs, shuffling papers, or fiddling with a pencil. In fact, when a customer is behaving in this way, I acknowledge it. I say, "I can see that your mind is elsewhere. Is there a better time for us to talk or should we just barrel ahead?" Customers will respect your commitment and value to yourself because it reflects their own.

I also predict outcomes by identifying behaviors that are familiar to me from other people I've known: So-and-so sits like that; so-and-so was a doodler. I take good mental notes on people in the way I imagine actors do and for the same reason—because little details are where big truths reside. And truth is what sets a salesman free from anxiety about his or her future. I keep an index card file filled with salient details about each of my customers and prospects.

There's no shortage of consumer behavior theorists, by the way, who encourage salespeople to use a variety of psycho-physiological techniques to penetrate a customer's thinking, to study facial expressions, eye movements, body language, vocal tone. Some of what I've learned in the many, many seminars I've attended and books I've read has been an extension and validation of what I learned in the ghetto streets. But no one else values these skills enough to place them at the center of a seller's professional life the way I do. My insight has been to understand the wealth-making potential of the salesperson who is unique in the customer's professional life and experience.

This understanding has been crucial to my success, mental health, and career longevity. How effective would any football team be if every team in the league used the same playbook? Throughout the rest of this playbook we will talk about other surprising ways in which to differentiate yourself from your competition and make a lasting impression on a customer. You want your customer to become your *fan*, you see. Fans not only sing your praises to others, they refer you!

The Street-Smart Seven!

- Dress above standard with classic style.
- Make an indelible impression: Never bring materials on a first call. Just bring your brain.
- Devalue words, except as they are validated by behavior.
- Practice predicting outcomes by identifying customer behaviors that are familiar to you from other people you've known.

- When your feelings or suspicions are strong, acknowledge them, look for their source.

- Appreciate the wealth-making potential of a salesperson who is unique in the customer's professional life and experience.

- Turn your customer into your fan. Fans not only sing your praises to others, they refer you!

CHAPTER

9

A Sense of Urgency: Setting Priorities

The best thing about the future is that it comes only one day at a time.

—Abraham Lincoln

I never cease to be amazed at the difficulty salespeople have establishing daily work priorities. They actually appear to welcome distractions from the task at hand, the task of making money. Sales reps surf the web, gab on the phone, drink and linger at lunch with other sales reps, whine to each other about their bosses, the product line, and anything else. The only explanation for this time-wasting behavior I'm able to comprehend is that, unlike me, other people are confident of the future based on their good fortune in life so far. Otherwise, they would never fritter away precious moneymaking time recounting David Letterman's monologue or detailing the minutiae of management's shortcomings. If a salesperson wastes time in the way I describe, he or she grew up in another, much more forgiving universe than I did. What I live with is a compelling sense of *urgency*.

And it's urgency that helps me set my priorities. People like me, with a deep appreciation of the difference they can make through their own effort, understand the critical importance of mapping out a day's tasks toward a particular goal. The ability to know what's important and to set priorities accordingly is essential to success in any venture. If economics comes down to the choices made between alternatives in a world of scarcity, as the British economist Lionel Robbins observed back in 1932,[1] well then, in a place like East Harlem, a boy could hardly think or move too fast.

As far as I'm concerned, only one question should inform every moment in a salesperson's working life: *How much money am I making* (or *will I make*) *from this activity?* It doesn't matter what the specific activity is, whether it's a meeting, a phone call, product demonstration, computer upgrade, or research time. If you can translate the value of the activity into dollars and cents, the math will reveal all, and you will know where the task belongs on your to-do list.

Because the future politely arrives just one day at a time, as our sixteenth President so eloquently observed, I encourage the sales reps who work for me to be future-focused every morning and to begin the work day by writing down on an index card, by hand, six phone numbers with an odds-on chance of making the rep some money today. Though I have a laptop, an iPad, and a smartphone, nothing will ever render the pen and index card obsolete in my office. Use your hand-held by all means, but understand that the act of writing by hand, particularly in a small space like an index card, is a powerful one: How careful are you when filling out a blank form? Every number a Street-Smart salesperson writes in that space must be dialed that same day.

Try it! The pen-and-paper method is particularly useful when mapping a route to a potential major client to whom you have no other connection. Deals, like careers and like the future, are built one step at a time, and to land a big fish takes careful planning. Do your research. Map out your strategy on paper, phone call by inquiring phone call, and believe me, by the time you get face-to-face with Mr. Major Prospect, he will be impressed by: 1) your having identified him as a person of importance; 2) your determination to get his attention; 3) your understanding of the challenges and requirements of his business and the broader marketplace; and 4) his specific place in it all. Once again, you have distinguished yourself from other salespeople. Congratulations!

Plan, plan, and plan. Keep in mind that one of the greatest obstacles to success is an unrealistic goal. Make steady headway in achievable increments. In general, I advise that a sales rep telephone three prospects and three established customers every day. The prospecting calls are intended to generate interest, you understand, not immediate sales. With each and every call to a prospect, you're seeking two things: useful information and the opportunity to meet in person.

Calls to regular customers are different. *When you speak with a current client, the conversation has to bring value.* You're never calling a client to discuss last night's game, unless you know the game to be that person's passion. Once you've known a customer for some time, it's easy to bring value to even the briefest conversation. In fact, brevity can be a very powerful motivator: This offer expires at noon Friday! You don't have to act right now, but if you want to learn more, give me a call back.

Before dialing, consult your notes and be sure to tailor your message to reflect your client's personality and buying history. If your customer is all about money, let him know right away that you're calling with a thought you had that could boost his income. It goes without saying that you will be able to provide details when he asks, as he surely will. If your customer is a glutton for flattery, shower him with a little praise (not too much!) in the form of a suggestion that would put another feather in his cap, perhaps make him the envy of his colleagues. If productivity floats his boat, wow him with new product-performance statistics. If she's a stickler for details, address some inadequate aspect of the servicing of her account before she thinks of it. But always, always, say as little as possible; be tantalizing, not overtly controlling. Remember, the more a customer reveals about himself over time, the merrier: He hath anointed you a lifetime healer.

So many salespeople call up a customer just to shoot the breeze. They think that by talking about something other than business they are showing the customer that they aren't just after his money. Nothing should be further from the truth and the customer knows it, so don't interrupt his day with nothing in particular to say. He will not be flattered or reassured—just bothered. In my experience, far from being non-threatening, business conversations devoid of purpose make a customer feel like he or she is being set up, delivering a two-steps-backward result. Small talk is no way of bonding with your customers; they know that salespeople are not really friend material. And the last thing a Street-Smart salesman wants is to be lumped in a customer's category of phony salespeople. Don't pretend friendship. If you're not after your customer's money, what are you after? You're a salesperson! It's your mind-reading and problem-solving abilities that keep you in a customer's value equation, not your good looks or sense of humor or love of sailing or anything else, although such things can play a role. Every communication must have obvious business value to the client. I can't overemphasize this point. In fact, I want to elaborate.

The Street-Smart Seven!

- Only one question should inform every moment in a salesperson's workday: How much money am I making (or will I make) from this activity?

- Begin the workday by writing down on an index card, *by hand*, six phone numbers with an odds-on chance of making you some money today, ideally three prospects and three clients. Every number must be dialed that same day.

- To land a big fish takes careful planning. Do your research. Map out your strategy on paper, phone call by inquiring phone call. By the time you reach your prospect, he may well have heard of you—and be flattered by your intention to speak with him.

- Avoid unrealistic goals. Chart your progress in achievable increments.

- Always consult your notes on a client before dialing.

- Phone conversations with clients must bring value. Be brief, tantalizing. You're busy, too!

- Don't pretend friendship with a client. If you're not after your customer's money, what are you after? You're a salesperson!

10

The Role of Emotion

What people call impartiality may simply mean indifference, and what people call partiality may simply mean mental activity.

—G. K. Chesterton

At the start of a business call, you may briefly talk sports, family, weather, sure. But keep in mind that your duty is to be a trouble-free, problem-solving constant in a customer's working life. You'll fill that role best if you never forget that every conversational exchange, no matter how apparently casual, is, for you, a purposeful, fact-finding mission. You don't need your customer to talk baseball with you—you can talk baseball *in a way you care about* with your friends. What you're pursuing is a customer's business; you're just using baseball stories and other commonalities to probe for useful information. What's important to your baseball-loving customer? Stats? Paydays? Tradition? Honor? Loyalty? Let him lead; whatever he reveals, keep it in mind when structuring a deal for him. Because people buy on emotion, not logic.

The thoughtfulness you display toward a client must never be interpretable as false camaraderie. A professional is able to confer his attention without being perceived as looking for a friend. In my entire career, I have never had a client say to me in the spirit of friendship, "Hey, profits are up and I want to increase the price I pay to you for the goods." That's fairy-tale stuff. So don't feign a shared interest in small planes just because you see a couple of framed pictures behind a client's desk. You can only inquire about his interest in flying machines so long as your interest is sincere and you pay close attention to his remarks. If you happen to spark a client to talk freely about his hobby you will learn useful things about him, revelations you can use to your mutual benefit. But don't pretend to knowledge you don't have. Your client will then correctly read you as desperate and pandering, both serious turn-offs.

Regardless of whether or not you genuinely like him or her, there is nevertheless no such thing as a highly remunerative long-term *emotional* relationship with a client—do not look for one. Once emotions enter into the sales equation, everything is up in the air. You can have a blow-up with a spouse without ending the marriage, but as soon as emotions explode with a customer, no matter how long you've been doing business, the relationship is at risk.

When I was a kid, I grew sadly accustomed to feeling completely alone in the world for at least part of every day. At times, not caring what people thought, or not having anybody know where I was, felt oddly liberating. I could do whatever I wanted or had to do. My particular path to self-reliance is nothing I would wish on anybody, and I'm grateful for the strong moral compass I was given and still have. But as a consequence of my childhood isolation I'm able to experience a customer's personal ambivalence toward me as a net plus—because it allows me to adopt whatever stance will prove most effective in the situation, and to keep my hitter's eye on my bottom line, where it belongs. I recommend that you adopt the same clear-eyed perspective. Value and performance are the keys to success in our profession, not love and affection. Emotions undercut profits. It's as simple as that.

Who will pay you the best price for your car when you decide to sell it? Your brother? Your friend? A stranger? Emotional bonds inhibit even talk of buying and selling; it's just too uncomfortable. Getting people to like you should be the foundation of your human existence in the same way that getting out of bed is the foundation of your business enterprise. No less than that.

The need for approval, not just friendship, confuses personal relationships and is likewise always toxic in sales. Approval seeking undermines your focus on the deal under discussion with ill-defined, uncomfortable, and unproductive thoughts. Your minutes and seconds with a customer are limited. The less time you waste establishing how uncannily alike you are and the kismet that brought you into each other's lives, the more time you can spend gathering the useful information that will help you shape a deal the customer cannot sanely refuse—because the deal addresses his *pain* (everybody's in pain, you know), his dissatisfactions, his aspirations.

On the rare occasion that you land a client who desires your love and approval, you may begin to count your blessings. Folks who can't help telling you more about themselves than they realize will tell you everything you need to know to part them from more and more of their company's money. The emotionally needy client has no interest in your travel history; he's talking about his vacation because that's his way of feeling on top. Your task is to take note of what he remembers best, what he brags about, all that he wishes he had more time to do.

And never burst such a customer's bubble! Let him tell you how to treat his pain instead. Encourage him with enthusiastic questions that serve your business interests. Ask: "What would allow you to feel as good about yourself at work as you do when you're kayaking?" Get it? Understand that buying is driven by emotion and that *a buying decision is the only good place for emotion in a selling relationship*. What sells a house? Is it the boiler room? The insulation? With the price of oil, you'd think these would be driving considerations. But they aren't. It's the kitchen with a breakfast nook, the view from the master bedroom, the landscaping, the pool, all the things that allow the buyer to feel good about his or her achievements in life and fantasize about the coming rewards.

A customer's freely offered off-topic enthusiasms are best used to get him to open up about the pressure he feels at his desk—who is breathing down his neck from management; why exactly he's talking to you instead of to a competitor or even his current vendor. Ask follow-up questions to points he's already raised. Ask him to be specific about what's most pressing, most important to him at this moment. Once you identify the source(s) of his pain—professional, aspirational—you will be able to heal them. But in small doses! Allow time for your value to a customer to mount so that he becomes loyal and even dependent upon you.

■ ■ ■

Speaking of longevity, let me say something I shouldn't have to say to a professional. Longevity is underpinned by attentive servicing to the account that goes beyond making sure deliveries happen when they're supposed to. Even the most highly compensated salespeople can fall short in this aspect of the job. That's because high-performance types so richly appreciate the importance of steady prospecting that they can let it become too time-consuming. Prospecting is critical to the Street-Smart way of thinking, but must never be allowed to supersede client servicing on your daily list of priorities.

Street-Smart selling requires that you keep an eye on your people; otherwise they wander off and get into trouble. Just as my overwhelmed father had other eyes on us kids, create your own network of hungry eyes and ears. Cultivate conversational relationships with secretaries, employees, administrators. These are the people who know what's going on at street level. And they appreciate it when someone acknowledges the value of their perspective!

A quiet customer, you see, is not necessarily a happy customer. Check in with customers regularly and use a light touch that, again, brings *value*. Read an interesting article online? E-mail it to clients you know will find it interesting. See an ad for a wristwatch you're sure a client would like? Send her the link, not the watch. Wordless, thoughtful, and unexpected hellos play a very useful role in building longevity, efforts that make an impression but don't require a response. Use Google alerts on different topics to make sure you hear the latest news about topics relevant not only to your industry, but to your clients.

In my world, client services extend well beyond routine, half-sincere follow-up calls to make sure everything is performing as advertised. Client services should let a customer know not only that her business is appreciated, but should reassure her that the interest you take in the specifics of her situation is sincere. Without fanfare, I keep track of various details about my clients as they arise, and without being intrusive: e-mail and home addresses, family members, birthdays, illnesses, hobbies, likes and dislikes. I used to send a highly anticipated first class cheesecake to good clients on their birthdays. For a few years I gave out lottery tickets, too. In particular, ancillary staff greatly appreciate lottery tickets because they know you could be giving up a winner. Odds are you aren't, of course, but what a memorable gesture! What you want is to make the most impact with the least possible work. If some assistant hits the Lotto on a card you gave him, so be it. He'll sure be talking about you in the newspapers.

The Street-Smart Seven!

- There is no such thing as a profitable long-term emotional relationship with a client: Do not look for one! Be a problem-solving constant in your customer's professional life.

- People buy on emotion, not logic!

- A buying decision is the only good place for emotion in a selling relationship.

- On the rare occasion that you land a client who desires *your* love and approval, you may begin to count your blessings in dollars—quietly and to yourself.

- A quiet customer is not necessarily a happy cus-tomer: Check in regularly with your clientele,

---

but always with a reason that brings value to the conversation.

- Professional longevity is best served by attentiveness that goes beyond making sure deliveries happen on time.
- Build client profiles discreetly, keeping track of various details as they arise. Don't pry!

CHAPTER

11

Abandon Hope!

Expectation is the root of all heartache.
—William Shakespeare

In East Harlem, hope, with an implied capital H, was a major coin of the realm. Everybody was selling it: politicians, priests, wiseguys, dealers, do-gooders, everybody. But you can't, of course, eat *Hope* for dinner or use it to pay bills. I never put much stock in Hope because my survival was so obviously at stake every day. Instead, I was alert to opportunities and dismissive of promises.

I once asked one of my reps why he was spending several hours a week conducting staff education seminars for a prospect without any commitment to buy our products. His answer, in essence, was that he hoped his selflessness and generosity would move the prospect to do business with him.

He hoped. He didn't believe; he didn't trust; he didn't *know*. He hoped. Hear me now: *Hope is the enemy of success in sales!* When a customer suggests that if you help him by providing something for free he will use your products at some time in the future, don't consider it any kind of victory. He's yanking your chain, making hollow promises in exchange for getting something out of you for free in the here and now. He's a better salesperson than you.

Here's what a hollow promise sounds like: "Come back and see me when you have the upgrade," or, "Looks good—I'll call you after my committee meeting." Do you—dare you—hope that this customer means what he says? Not if you're a Street-Smart salesman.

If a customer is trying to sell you futures it means you haven't penetrated to the source of his motivation to buy *today*. He doesn't see any value in your relationship at this moment and is trying to get rid of you as productively for him as possible—in this case, by pretending to leave the door open. It may be true that some product modification or service improvement one day will make a difference to him and you'll be sure to call him on that happy occasion. But right now? Turn the tables on him and be blunt. Say: "I am encouraged by your comments and I'm happy to circle back to you in the future. But I have to say that, usually, when prospects tell me to come back they are just being polite, because I did a lousy job of explaining the benefits of working with us today." Expect silence.

Then, because it is human nature to want to fix things, the prospect will say something to try to alleviate your pain in any way. In so doing, he will tell you all about what motivates him to buy *today*. Congratulations. You have performed a Street-Smart information extraction!

Would you dare, though? He won't be expecting you to challenge him, I promise you. And that's good, because it helps you distinguish yourself from other salespeople he's dealt with. Let him come up with an answer to your question, and be prepared to press him when he tries to get away with rephrasing what he already said.

Pursue a real answer. As sellers, our job is to figure a way to bring value to the immediate circumstance. A seller represents many products, after all. If your customer is truly focused on technical details, point him to the high performers in your kitbag. If he's only interested in fire sales, sell him surplus goods for now but make it an obvious effort on his behalf. Whatever information you gather from him at this early point in the sales cycle will be useful every time you call this customer or profile another like him.

This is an important point, especially in instances where the product or company a seller represents does not have market share. What is your differentiator in such a situation? The Street-Smart salesman is a student of human nature. That is why I recommend you read books on human psychology. The lessons of one business relationship or transaction may be extended to any number of others. If you find that one client's behavior reminds you of another's or of your Uncle Pete, pay attention to that. It's meaningful and there's a reason for it. Figure out what it is and factor it in.

My rep's hope-based behavior was, sadly, not at all unusual. I hear this kind of logic from reps at every experience level and it's hardly surprising when you consider that conventional wisdom encourages product giveaways as way stations on the tricky path to the wallet. But, I ask you, freebies as the *first* step? Does that make any sense? Why would you start a battle (as many, myself included, approach the sales cycle) with a little surrender?

"Free" is the most powerful word in an advertiser's vocabulary, but can be the most costly in a salesperson's lexicon, especially in business-to-business transactions, where "free" always suggests weakness. Sales professionals have been programmed to think they are behaving rationally, even being a devilish bit calculating, with the freebies they dispense so grandly at the outset and the ease with which they cultivate phony friendships. But from my perspective, this kind of behavior is utterly irrational. Handouts signal neediness and play directly into deeply ingrained stereotypes of the desperate salesman. Worse still, by giving away handouts you fail to differentiate yourself from the competition even as you insist that your products are better than theirs. It doesn't make any sense. Try to get a freebie from Apple!

If your time, expertise, insight, product samples, and more have no value to you, why should a customer pay top dollar for them? Once a client knows he can get something for nothing from you, even if he does do business with you, there's no way he's ever going to pay premium. And premiums are how the high-performance salesperson makes real money. You must eliminate hope from the selling equation.

■ ■ ■

Trusting that something *is* going to happen is, for me, far more unsettling than knowing for sure that something is *not* going to happen. Trusting—blind faith—hope—lead to taking the rest of the day off and spending money you have yet to earn. I relearned that lesson in an instant way back when I was starting out and first beginning to do well.

I was browsing in Ralph Lauren's shop on Madison Avenue, daring to feel pretty good about my prospects and myself. I had one really big client plus a few smaller ones, and I was taking in about $30,000 a month in commissions. I had nothing in the pipeline, however, not a single, solitary prospect. I was weighing the appeal of several silk ties when I got a mobile phone call that cost me 70 percent of my business and about 60 percent of my income. I'd been twice underpriced by the competition, lost my two biggest customers, and my monthly income had fallen to $12,000. On top of that, I'd made the mistake of not having enough business in the pipeline.

Such a thing had not happened to me before and has not happened since. That's because I never again allowed myself to depend on existing business and, at least as important, never again allowed lower price to be reason enough for a client to quit me. The tangible value I determined always to bring to my clients has made me difficult to easily replace.

A lot of the mediocre salespeople who competed against me back then assessed my relentless pursuit of new prospects as naked greed, as in, "Wow, Belli's never satisfied." My inability to participate in small talk with them didn't help my image either, and I understood how they could see me the way they did. But it wasn't greed that drove me, and it sure wasn't hope. It was *fear*, a first-class motivator all of its own. My pursuit of Sister and a diploma arose from fear, didn't it, but it turned out to be the first in a series of actions I took that changed my life for the better.

I resolved henceforth to leave as little of my destiny to chance as possible. I doubled and redoubled my daily efforts; I was the cold calling-est rep on the sales force. In three months I rebuilt my business to previous levels, this time with one major difference: I now kept so many new opportunities before me that I could work day and night all week and weekends too, and still not get to them all. Perhaps I overcompensated, given my background. Find your own balance, but always be pushing the envelope.

I want everyone to have hope for the future. I do. I'm just a realist and a pragmatist. I don't want you ever to lose sight of what I know for sure: that you can't be sure what will happen next year, next week, even a minute from now. That's a hard truth and we all live with it in our way. Poverty taught me that a person can never have too many options and that it's better, safer to have too many options than too few. I'm not anti-hope, you understand, I'm anti-wishful thinking. I favor the kind of hope that incorporates the understanding that the quality of our lives has everything to do with our personal actions. Continuous prospecting is a major way a high-performance salesperson keeps hope alive.

The Street-Smart Seven!

- Hope is the enemy of success in sales and leads to taking the rest of the day off and spending money you have yet to earn.

- Never allow price to be reason enough for a client to quit you.

- If a customer is trying to sell you futures, it means you haven't penetrated to the source of his motivation to buy *today*.

- Freebies as the first step? Why would you start a battle with a little surrender?

- If your time, expertise, insight, product samples, and more have no value to you, no customer will ever pay top dollar for them.

- When a customer suggests that if you provide something for free he will use your products at some time in the future, he's yanking your chain.

- Continuous prospecting is how a sales rep sleeps at night. There is no such thing as having too many options.

CHAPTER

12

Charming Strangers: Prospecting

I do not seek. I find.

—Pablo Picasso

Who is a prospect? Broadly, a prospect is the decision maker at a company who buys the kinds of things you have to sell, hasn't met you, may or may not have heard of you or your company, and may or may not become your customer. Most important, a prospect presents an array of moneymaking possibilities that allow a high-performance salesperson to sleep well at night.

128

My concept of prospecting is the pursuit of someone I did not know yesterday who will help me earn money tomorrow. For the sake of health and well-being every bit as much as for dollars and cents, sales professionals need to cultivate a steady, career-long parade of *potential* clients. Remember: Regular customers, no matter how many, are not everything. Having a dance card crowded with new names is what removes doubt and anxiety from your voice and neediness from your behavior, leveling the playing field and putting your prospect at ease.

Only steady prospecting delivers the self-confidence that enables you to charge above-average prices pursuant to my interpretation of the Law of Supply and Demand: Plenty of customers (demand) plus limited supply (my time and attention) equal the right for me to charge premium prices. After all, if I'm not charging premium, how am I going to decide which of my many clients to dote upon? Clients who pay premium get extra attention. They know it and expect it. They're willing, even happy, to pay for it, too, if the rewards are good enough.

The reason prospecting is such a powerful engine to a sales business is that prospecting gives a rep *options*. Options are a steroid for competitiveness, and competitiveness generates energy to be turned back into prospecting. It's a Street-Smart cycle. When I say, "Never enough," I'm not talking about greed, I'm talking about winning. We don't say that ballplayers are greedy because they get so many hits or baskets, or that scientists are greedy because they have so many discoveries. But when a similar level of achievement is applied to business and the currency is money instead of home runs, success can be labeled as greed. However, no one begrudges the fortune of a responsible businessperson who is honest in his or her dealings and demonstrably civic-minded.

Here's the thing. *The Street-Smart Salesman is 20 percent farmer and 80 percent hunter.* Can you understand that? Give good time to the task of sniffing out new blood every day. The confidence you'll gain from having such a busy calendar will keep your fires stoked.

The key to effective prospecting is to focus on the user. The product user drives the yes and no. True, there may be administrators, purchasing agents, buyers, or others with some level of involvement. But in business-to-business sales, the user has the greatest influence on the outcome. So, seek out users, the so-called *influencers* in the buying equation, prospects who may or may not be buyers themselves, but nevertheless may have significant influence over those in a position to buy. Find these folks! Once you have a product's users on your side, they will lobby the purchasing agents for you. The users who actually handle the products you're selling are in many ways the most powerful advocates for the Street-Smart seller in his dealings with buyers.

Likewise, *gatekeepers* can prove significant allies. Gatekeepers are the people at a company who have decision-making power over what information makes it to the executive you need to convert. Receptionists rule! Secretaries and assistants cull! They decide which calls get through, manage the executive's calendar, and prioritize information. Most salespeople regard gatekeepers as obstacles, expenses, and liabilities. We don't. We recognize them as a portal onto the buying system of their company. Treat the gatekeepers with the same respect as their bosses—and work them as effectively, too.

If you find yourself having to sell to a committee, which happens a small percentage of the time, make every effort to meet face-to-face with each member prior to the joint session. Avoid conference calls. The technical pitfalls are many, and while your ability to observe and exploit personal behaviors may be reduced in a room full of people, it is denied over the telephone.

If you must sell to a committee without any prior one-on-ones, to the best of your ability *profile* each committee member with a mind to discover something about what motivates him or her. Identify your possible champion(s); maybe let your champion know that you're no good at the bureaucratic game (even though you are), and ask him or her to help you out when the big day comes.

When making the appointment to meet with a committee, ask for clarification of the purpose of the meeting and, every bit as important, what will happen after the meeting is over. This is an essential detail. Typically, unless you ask for a decision at meeting's end, they'll all want to go off and talk among themselves and get back to you. In truth, committee meetings are a corporate fail-safe tactic intended to stall, or at least slow, the momentum toward money changing hands. Resist submitting to a company's vaunted "process" as courteously as you can, for the glacial pace of that process is not to your advantage. Profitable companies are never eager to switch vendors, you see. They prefer the stability of the status quo.

When you do find yourself having to sell to a committee in person, pay attention to everyone in the room as best you can. Be sure to ask a lot of well-formed questions at the start. Why? Because as soon as you do, a leader will emerge from the group and the game is on. Observe the dynamics between the players at the table. Don't fixate on the apparent power person, and don't let the more timid members defer to him. Empower the quieter voices by soliciting their opinions; your profile of such a person should have given you reason to trust that what he'll say will be of benefit. You also may discover that their opinion is highly valued and could play a consequential part in the follow-up meetings they are accustomed to having.

Above all, be prepared for anything. Buyers at any level appreciate, and will more likely reward, a sales presentation that reflects a thorough knowledge of their particular company and the field in general. What they do not appreciate, I assure you, is having a sales rep run down the competition, especially their current vendor. Never so much as mention the competition. You are not like them and they are not your concern. Your sale is based on *your* solution to the customer's problem and how it advances that customer's vision of personal success.

■ ■ ■

The best prospects, needless to say, come about through referrals, recommendations from satisfied customers. A referred prospect is the gold standard in sales, as close to an automatic deal as you can get on a first call. Think of your own purchases, big or small. Was there an "opinion leader" who influenced your decision? A trusted relative, friend, or co-worker who vouched for the person or product? That's very often the case.

Nevertheless, some (too many) sales reps are loath to approach even their steadiest customer for a referral. They fear rocking the boat, asking too much and triggering a rejection. This fear arises, mind you, despite the fact that the average sales rep is likely to describe himself as a friend of his best customer. But, believe me, if a "satisfied" customer declines to refer you to a colleague, you already have a problem you're not acknowledging. This would be a good time to find out what it is.

New York City's former mayor, Ed Koch, used to get a lot of mileage out of asking, "How'm I doing?" When you ask a customer for a referral, you're raising the same underlying question. Don't be afraid of the answer, whatever it is, just respond to it productively. Make it a practice to pursue one referral from each of your clients annually, if only to test the current status of your relationship. Some customers, you will find, actually like to be asked for a referral, welcoming your request as a validation of their status and authority.

Before you pop the question, however, demonstrate that you have done your homework, just as you always do.

The request to make of your customer is not, "Do you know anybody else who would like to meet with me?" but "Can you help me out with an introduction to Mr. Chuck Jones at The Acme Company?" I estimate that upwards of 80 percent of the time a solid customer of a Street-Smart seller will gladly make a specific call on your behalf.

In general, as I'm sure you've noticed—and having nothng to do with business—people don't like to ask for favors. Salespeople are hardly unique in their reluctance to ask for referrals. Yet we're all in need of a little assistance from time to time, aren't we? And we're supposed to pull ourselves up by our bootstraps, aren't we? Requests for referrals occupy a time-honored place in the world of Getting Ahead. Remember, all you're asking of your well-serviced client is a vote of confidence, not a line of credit. You're building your company, creating enterprise, just as your customer is. A request for a recommendation telegraphs ambition, momentum, and determination. And the specificity of your goal (to meet Mr. Jones at Acme) is evidence of a business plan in action. These are qualities a high-performing client can appreciate and identify with.

Be advised that the customer who declines to recommend you not only has a problem with you, but may also be talking (and getting closer) to the competition. Again, you must address any refusal to recommend you immediately. The moment you are turned down, say something along these lines. "Joe, it's clear I shouldn't have put you in that position, but please help me to understand why you're reluctant to call Mr. Jones on my behalf." Your next move will depend on his explanation. But you must try to uncover the truth. There is no running away from bad reviews. Listen to and deal with bad news immediately and at the source. By the time bad news reaches the proverbial grapevine, it'll be too late to counter it. Trust enough in your reality-based relationship with a customer to know that pretty much any issue he raises can be resolved.

The Street-Smart Seven!

- Cultivate a steady, career-long parade of *potential* clients. A crowded dance card removes anxiety from your voice and neediness from your behavior.

- Identify and target...
  - *influencers*, particularly users, and other non-buyers who may have influence over those in a position to buy;
  - *gatekeepers*, people with power to decide which information makes it to the attention of the executive you need to convert. Receptionists rule! Secretaries and assistants cull!

- Avoid committees and conference calls whenever possible. Face-to-face is where the action is!

- If you must, *before* you sell to a committee...
  - ask for clarification of the purpose of the meeting and what will happen at its conclusion;

(continued)

(continued)

- to the best of your ability, *profile* each committee member and identify your most likely champion(s).

- *While* selling to a committee . . .
  - don't fixate on the apparent power person, and don't let the more timid members defer to him or her. Empower quieter voices by soliciting opinions. Never denigrate the competition.

- Ask your customers for referrals to specific individuals about once a year. When you ask a customer for a referral, you're really asking, "How'm I doing?" Don't be afraid of the answer; just respond to it productively.

- If a customer declines to refer you, you have a problem you're not acknowledging. Said customer is probably already talking to the competition. Listen to and deal with bad news immediately and at the source. There is no running away from bad reviews, just as there is no crying in baseball.

CHAPTER

13

A Minute to Live: Cold Calling

Apart from the known and the unknown, what else is there?

—Harold Pinter

You may have been surprised to hear me say that salespeople, even above average salespeople, do not prospect often or creatively enough, but it's true. And it's true because salespeople are generally intimidated by the idea of having to talk to strangers. In this fear, salespeople are not unlike most people; they're just in a job that requires them to get over it! One of the most valuable assets a salesperson can have is the ability to acquire business in tough times. Cold calling is an essential skill when business is slow that also must be exploited when business is good.

People in need of approval from others regard the cold call, in and of itself, as an act of desperation and a harbinger of personal tragedy. And though there's a huge territory between making a cold call and being Willie Loman, you wouldn't know it by most reps' behavior. The prospect of making a cold call conjures a crushing self-doubt in many, too many, of them. The characters in Mamet's *Glengarry Glen Ross* constitute a rogue's gallery of desperate, predatory dialers, stereotypes that tap deep-rooted suspicions about salespeople—perhaps most deeply *among* salespeople!

Because so many reps recoil from cold calling, entire salesforces lavish their attention on core customers with the reasonable expectation—in the hope—that their generosity will engender new business down the pike and that they will pick up a new client here and there as time goes marching on. There is much to be said for being attentive to a good client and, as I've told you, not all reps are. But, to put it bluntly, you simply can't make big money in sales without cold calling.

When I started out selling life insurance, I was given a Westchester (New York) County phone book, pencil, paper, and instructions to "Start with the letter A." Other reps had other phone books. As a novice, I couldn't believe that such a huge company would have so much riding on cold calls; there were a lot of us working the phones and the company spent quite a bit of money and time training and outfitting each of us. With time, I came to see that the company had done their cost-effectiveness homework regarding the best use of their sales team. The company had a lot riding on cold calls, and they still do, and they always will. That's because the math is on the side of the cold caller.

Very few salespeople grasp this golden nugget because they have so little experience of the truth of it, but the arithmetic is simple. Here goes: If a salesperson has no prospects but makes ten cold calls that generate two appointments, she has increased her chances of making a new sale by 20 percent. Right? But most salespeople, like most people, simply can't handle the prospect of getting nowhere eight out of ten times. With my background, I'm not one of them. I can handle rejection; I've handled way worse situations than having someone hang up on me: I lived through my high school guidance counselor telling me I stank, didn't I? I'm willing to bet you've also handled tougher, even more embarrassing situations than a hang-up from a stranger. Everyone gets knocked down; the key is getting back up. Ted Williams failed to get on base about 65 percent of the time. But what everyone remembers is what he did the other 35 percent of the time.

Adopt a Street-Smart seller's persona and you can learn to handle cold calling, too. The rewards are too great not to learn how to do it well. You can and should make thousands of cold calls over the course of your career—all the while retaining a positive self-image. Relax! Pick up a phone and have some fun! People are fascinating. Put yourself in your listener's shoes; try out different approaches. Turn selling into a game and get good at it. No matter what, keep a steady pace. Don't slack off only to find yourself making no money this month and having to start dialing. Your anxiety will tell in your voice. Dial for dollars every day and your concern for your future will melt away, lending a relaxed quality to your voice that only improves your odds of landing an appointment.

When I made my first cold calls, I was amazed *any* time I got an appointment, much less made a sale. Because I was genuinely curious about what caused one person to hear me out and another to hang up, I kept track of every call, names, addresses, age, ethnicity, and so on, looking for patterns. Sometimes it was my simple curiosity that kept a prospect on the line; they could hear it in my voice.

I also made time to drive around the neighborhoods I was cold calling, observing how the people there lived, what mattered to them, what they aspired to. I won't say that I loved cold calling, but I dove in and made it work for me. These people were from another, upscale world! As long as I learned as much as I could during every call, I considered that I was making progress. And what do you know, as I began to understand the needs, aspirations, and concerns of complete strangers in Westchester, New York, I was able to customize deals that enabled me to sell a million dollars' worth of insurance in my first year, right out of the phone book.

Let me make one more observation about the phone book. Nowadays, call lists are scientific, demographic, psychographic, behavioral profiles intended to identify (isolate) the types of people who buy certain products. The crudely alphabetical list of Westchester county residents thrown on my desk 30 years ago was in some way a gift to a person like me accustomed to working with limited resources. That's when I'm at my most creative. The results spoke for themselves.

Some of my colleagues used to open every cold call with the line, "This call is not about selling you anything." Technically, it was true, but, technically, it was also a lie. A lie for an opening line! That wasn't going to work for me. I approached every call as a 60-second opportunity to earn someone's trust, someone who didn't know me and couldn't see me. I tried to hear myself as they were hearing me. In general, I found it was best to be bright-eyed and straightforward—just as I am in real life—and to be clear with people about what I wanted up front. A cold call doesn't last long enough to allow for much nuance. It's nakedly an opportunity hunt.

I want to say something here about "opportunism" because salespeople tend to be hypersensitive to the characterization. Opportunism refers to business deals conducted for reasons of self-interest invisible to, and therefore unpredictable by, the other party. There is nothing inherently devious about the pursuit of self-interest. In particular, by providing solutions to one or more aspects of a customer's pain, Street-Smart deals are *mutually* rewarding, highly remunerative to both sides of the sales equation and thus immune to any moral scrutiny.

To my mind, opportunism is better understood as opportunity *seeking*, the mandate in the sales trade. The ability to act quickly when an opportunity arises is a prerequisite for success in anything—overcoming poverty, growing a business, getting the girl/guy, anything. It's certainly nothing to be ashamed of. Good card players don't cheat; they keep track, play odds, ever alert to opportunity. Somebody calls you an opportunist? Smile... because you are!

One final word on cold calling, and it's a bit of advice that actually extends beyond that specific circumstance to your overall professional life. Never thank anyone for "taking the time to talk to" you. Ever. People use parting phrases like "Thanks for your time" in a reflexive, unconsidered way. They think it sounds polite. But think about it again. Never thank anyone for "taking the time to talk to" you. In my world, a high-performance salesperson's time is every bit as valuable as her customer's and almost surely pays better. When parting with a customer, whether in person or on the phone, say, "Thanks, Jane. That was a [helpful, fascinating, productive] conversation. I look forward to our speaking again." Keep the playing field level and the door open wide.

If you get through your opening on a cold call—and mostly you will not—and the prospect nevertheless indicates that she is not interested in what you're selling, accept the decision graciously along these lines: "I didn't

think you'd be interested, since this is a random call."
Then, before the line goes dead, try to squeeze in a
question like this: "But can I ask how you generally
get information about new products?" You really want
to know! If you get an answer, you will have gained
a foothold. Congratulations! Now work your way back
to business and re-pitch, from a more promising angle,
incorporating all you've learned about your prospect in
the last few seconds. Ready, go!

■ ■ ■

The Street-Smart Seven!

- You can't make big money in sales without cold
  calling. Regard the telephone as your friend and
  resource.

- Know that the math is on the side of the cold
  caller: If a rep makes 10 calls that generate two
  appointments, she has increased her chances of a
  new sale by 20 percent. Right?

- Most salespeople (like most people) simply can't
  handle the prospect of getting nowhere eight out
  of ten times. Don't be like most people.

- No matter what, keep a steady pace. Don't slack
  off only to find yourself making no money this
  (continued)

(continued)

month and having to start dialing. Your anxiety will tell in your voice.

- Research the people you're phoning: Who are they? What do they want from life?
- Every cold call is a 60-second opportunity to earn someone's trust, someone who doesn't know you and can't see you. Try to hear yourself as you are speaking: What would keep *you* from hanging up? Have some fun! People are fascinating.
- Never thank anyone for "taking the time to talk to" you. To do so only devalues your time and expertise.

14

What's Fair Is Fair

Quid pro quo, Agent Starling.

—Hannibal Lecter

A prospect wants something from my rep: training for her office staff. Said prospect knows that additional staff training will enhance her business in some meaningful way—and my rep knows it, too. Here we have an ideal situation in which to look for the fair exchange, the *quid pro quo*, which translates from Latin as "something for something," or "this for that."

Listen closely to how a Street-Smart seller lays out the terms of a *quid pro quo*: "Mary, whenever I conduct training seminars *for my customers* [note the emphasis], the jump in staff confidence that follows translates directly into enhanced customer service. Improved customer service then boosts word of mouth referrals. Before we get into specifics today, please help me understand how my investment of time and resources to improve your staff's performance will affect our business relationship."

A very reasonable inquiry! And you've actually used *two* Street-Smart tactics in so doing. One, you've made it clear that you don't give anything away *except to a customer*. Two, you appear to have handed control of the conversation by giving a customer the opportunity to propose a suitable structure for your business relationship. Your customer is not expecting this; I guarantee it. Her response will vary depending on the kind of person she is and her circumstances. If what she then proposes is consistent with your goals, agree to it, *slowly*. Remember, the Street-Smart seller solves problems in small doses in order to build customer loyalty. If her response is not consistent with your goals, be clear about what would make the difference for you, what would get *you* to "Yes."

Buyers are completely unaccustomed to being asked to define their relationship with a seller, so don't be surprised if at first you draw an evasive response along the lines of, "Well, I guess if I like what I see, maybe in the future we can do some business." But as a matter of routine, the "hope-less" Street-Smart seller never settles for future-based promises. All future-based promises—and I mean *all*—are nothing more than stall tactics with the ultimate goal of getting rid of you forever. I guarantee you, whatever circumstance this customer claims would cause him to open his wallet will have changed the next time you speak with him because circumstances will have changed. You won't be in the room, for instance.

Anytime I hear the "maybe-if" equation uttered, my ghetto radar starts beeping loudly. It is not in my professional skill set to believe in future-based promises and it shouldn't be in yours. At such moments—not later in the day or the next day, but right then—it's very important that you be clear with your customer about your problem with her response. Say what you have to say without changing the tone of your voice and becoming defensive. Without hesitation or provocation, point out that the customer is asking for a significant investment on your part for possibly no financial return at all. Calmly remind the customer that professional business people *like us* (again, keep the playing field level) are understandably reluctant to donate energy and resources to an endeavor that conceivably could even end up benefiting the competition.

At such moments, locate your professional equilibrium in the knowledge that you are: (1), stating the obvious, and (2), that any request for an even exchange is by definition a reasonable one, indeed, the *most* reasonable one. Did I say don't get defensive? Don't! There's actually no need to. A single declaration of your point of view should be enough to turn the tide; it's something new under the moon. Give your words time to sink in. Scratch your head and look puzzled if you have to wait for an answer: Remember, you were only stating the obvious! Keep mum as long as you can without being rude, then, keeping the ball in the air, ask for clarity. Proceed along the lines of, "We're going to fix something that will help you with your business and you want me to do what?" Make sure the customer realizes that he's asking you to supply something highly valuable.

It's now likely, very likely (you won't believe how likely) that the customer will start to see her way clear to a mutually remunerative arrangement. Customers (people) don't want you to think they're being unfair or, more tellingly, that they don't know what they want. To create either impression wouldn't be in their interest. Once you withhold a freebie, a customer has to ask himself, "What's this guy got that makes him so reluctant to give it away?" Help him to ask you.

Everybody in East Harlem said they wanted to be fair with me—teachers, cops, guidance counselors, nuns, grocers, you name it. Leaving me to ask, "Why are so many things unfair around here if everyone wants to be fair with me?" Fairness is an ideal, but an ideal has very little specific relevance to the other party, to me or to you. The Street-Smart salesman wisely exploits this indefinable aspiration, helping a customer to give dollar and cents shape to his or her virtue.

Nobody wants to miss out on anything and everybody wants to associate with people who are a cut above the rest: the most skillful surgeon; the honest car mechanic; the Street-Smart seller. Take advantage of people's desire to surround themselves with the best. And what do you know? There's a very good chance that, now that she's seen that you take yourself and your profession seriously, this customer will end up paying a higher price for your goods and services than she might have had she not resisted you initially! That's Street-Smart selling.

If, as economist Milton Friedman observed and I agree, "There is no such thing as a free lunch," then long-term, highly remunerative selling relationships are unlikely to be born of giveaways. The Street-Smart seller trades not only in goods and services but in collective fantasy. Where the salesman's ideal scenario intersects with the customer's idea of the best deal possible, price is no longer an obstacle. Give a customer reason to think she's getting a certain, even unquantifiable, benefit or advantage by doing business with the likes of you, so obviously a cut above, and watch her pay happily for the privilege.

■ ■ ■

The Street-Smart Seven!

- When a client is looking to pay nothing for something—your time, for instance—say to him, "Before we get into specifics today, please help me understand how my investment of time and

(continued)

(continued)

resources to improve your staff's performance will affect our business relationship." Make sure the customer realizes that he's asking you to supply something highly valuable.

- Make it clear to your prospects that you don't give anything away except to a *customer*.

- Once you withhold a freebie, a customer has to ask himself, "What's this guy got that makes him so reluctant to give it away?" Help him to ask you.

- Future-based promises are nothing more than stall tactics with the goal of getting rid of you forever.

- Customers never want you to think they're being unfair or that they don't know what they want. Exploit such vanities!

- People want to avail themselves of the best of everything. Be unique in your style and approach and reap the rewards.

- Where the salesman's ideal scenario intersects with the customer's idea of the best deal possible, price is no longer an obstacle.

15

Ready, Set, Improvise: Using Visualization

Hindsight is always 20-20.

—Billy Wilder

Poor people often dream of being someone and somewhere else. I spent countless hours imagining myself in the Yankees dugout and out in centerfield. My self-image was entirely invested in such notions; no one could, or ever even tried, to convince me that the future held anything but baseball fame for me. Imagination is powerful stuff and visualization—the act and art of playing out a scenario in the privacy of your mind—is a very effective way to use the imagination to create a desired outcome. You can't use visualization to control a customer's behavior, of course. That would be magic. But for a Street-Smart salesman, visualization is serious business indeed, because it's a huge part of the difference between a daydream and a plan. Visualization, you could say, is daydreaming with intention.

Every high-performance athlete visualizes victory against specific opponents. Why? Because visualization is a powerful way of convincing yourself that you can win—because you have seen it happen in your mind's eye. Not once, but time after time! Repetition is key to unlocking the full power of visualization. The more often you envision yourself successfully navigating tough situations and getting to "Yes," the more at ease you will be when the time comes, the more comfortable you will be in the role of a high-performance salesperson.

Actors read and reread a script before they rehearse in three dimensions with other actors, in a room or on a bare stage. Interestingly, in order to best understand their character, some actors memorize the whole script, everybody's parts. I appreciate that, because sellers don't get to rehearse with buyers. For sellers to achieve the best possible results, every conceivable scenario must be conjured, rehearsed, in our heads beforehand. The kind of visualization I recommend involves taking time to sit quietly and create mental pictures of things both predictable and unpredictable that might occur during an upcoming appointment, and how you would best respond to each of those variables. Keep your eye on the prize at all times. Having a clear picture of what you want from an encounter ensures that you will make good choices as events proceed in reality.

What deal will you offer? Role-play various options in detail; discover what aspects of the deal you're willing to change and to what extent. Look at your notes on a customer; see her in your mind's eye. What is her office like? Is it noisy? Neat? Strewn with papers? Uncomfortably tidy? Picture it; put yourself in the room with her. Run numbers. Imagine the questions she might ask. What if your conversation is interrupted? What do you do? Always take time to switch perspectives, to look at and listen to yourself from your prospect's point of view. Are you fidgety? Composed? Talking too much? Are your shoes shined?

Before a Street-Smart seller gets into a conversation with a client, she will visualize, preview, and rehearse every conceivable (literally) aspect of the exchange. In that way we do our best to anticipate a client's professional and emotional needs, technical and financial concerns. We do not use our insights to finish a customer's sentences, though that can be occasionally effective if it's interpreted as mind reading, though you can be sure "mind readers" do a lot of rehearsing. If you've met the client before, review everything you've learned about her so far, her style, habits, social skills, preferences, fastidiousness, left-handedness—any and every detail that might affect the outcome of your meeting. The size of your payday may well depend on one or more of such details.

As you visualize the various directions a conversation might go, always concentrate on the underlying story, the one in which *you* get what you want. It goes without saying that the customer will get what she wants; you need to monetize *your* side of the equation. That's why you need to be the writer/director/star of the one-act plays you stage in your head. The more time you spend in this mode of proactive imagining, the better an improviser you'll become, with ready and effective responses to even unforeseen eventualities. As time goes on, you'll find that fewer and fewer things will even have the potential to throw you off your game. You will have seen it all before, either in person or on the high-definition screen in your head.

The goal of visualization is not, let me repeat, *not* to get to a place where you finish your client's sentences for him. The Street-Smart seller always resists the temptation to fill in a conversational blank unless absolutely certain that it's the best tactic in the circumstance. It's hard to keep quiet, I know. Salespeople, even our kind, are made uncomfortable by silence, too. But you can *learn to wait* and it's worth it to learn, because even an extra second can be long enough to prompt something useful.

Envision scenarios in which a particular client is slow to respond to a question. What do you do while you wait for your answer? What does he do? If you have to be the first to speak, what do you say? What feels like the most effective thing to do, or not to do, with this particular person? Be prepared for the wait! If you can do it, you will almost always learn something you wouldn't have learned otherwise; because you know your part so well, you're able to concentrate on what the customer is saying. And here's the bonus: You'll not only uncover exploitable information, you'll be improving the odds of a smooth closing. Because a customer who has spoken aloud about the deal he wants is a customer virtually certain to recognize the deal in print and sign the contract without hesitation.

The Power of Improvisation, *or Duct Tape to Win!*

Remember Uncle Steve from Chapter 1, the diehard alcoholic who hung out in the Belli kitchen? Here's the whole story. When I was 14, our apartment was burglarized about a half-dozen times. The last time, the locks on the door were so badly broken that they could not be cheaply replaced. The landlord was nowhere to be found—response time for a ghetto landlord can range from weeks to months to never. So there we were in one of the highest crime areas in New York in a tenement apartment without any locks on the only door. What did I do? I improvised a solution.

The first thing I did was ask two neighbors in the building, people I knew I could trust, to keep an eye and ear out. After that, because there's safety in numbers, I got my friends to hang out on my stoop instead of another one around the corner. I angled a kitchen chair under the doorknob at night and began sleeping with the radio on and leaving it on whenever the apartment was going to be undefended (I still leave the radio playing in my empty hotel room when I'm on the road). Eventually I got the idea to have the neighborhood drunk, the affable Uncle Steve, to make my kitchen his drinking headquarters. I loved the man anyway and it was a good deal for both of us: He got off the street and I got someone in the apartment all the time (*quid pro quo!*). For a finishing touch, I put a sign on the door reading "Nothing left but a fight."

We lived the next four years in our unlocked ghetto apartment without incident. That's the power of improvisation!

The Street-Smart Seven!

- Daydream with intention! Use visualization to see as clearly as you can into the future.

- Visualize meetings with clients before they happen with the intention of eliminating all possibility of surprise. Thorough mental preparation helps ensure you will make good choices as events proceed in reality.

- As you imagine the various directions an encounter might go, focus strongly on one or more scenarios that conclude with *you* getting what you want.

- Role-play the scene in your head in detail; discover which aspects of the deal you're willing to change and to what extent.

- The goal of visualization is not to finish a client's sentences for him, but to comprehend the forces at work and how they might play out.

- Visualization will improve the odds of a smooth closing.

- Remember: All high-performance athletes visualize victory. Repetition is important.

16

Defy Expectations

Do the opposite!

—George Costanza

Do you remember the great *Seinfeld* episode in which the erratically employed, perennially underachieving George Costanza goes on a job interview, having decided to act *against* his every lifelong instinct—and winds up with a dream job working for the New York Yankees? I love that episode. "Do the opposite!" becomes George's mantra. Next thing you know, the paunchy, bald man lands a date with a beautiful blonde by telling her in no uncertain terms that he's unemployed and living with his parents—instead of lying and pretending to be an architect, as he usually does. For once in his sorry life, Costanza is on to something: It can be very productive to do the opposite of everything you've been doing!

As I've said, all sales trainers instruct you to learn the script, *their* script, and stick to it or come running back to it, as the case may be. Me, I don't like scripts, and you won't find any in this book. Other selling systems seek to eliminate any need for improvisation on the salesman's part, but, as you know, I do the opposite. I like to live by my wits. Otherwise, where's the fun? Why would I want to work a job that's no fun? Do you?

Not long ago, one of my reps told me that I was the best salesperson he had ever seen. I was flattered, of course, but because I'm always looking to improve my game, I was genuinely curious as to why he thought so. He said, "Because when you win, it looks beautiful; and when you lose, it looks just as beautiful. You always look like you are having fun." He hit the nail right on the head. If you are not having fun working in sales, you are doing it all wrong!

From my perspective, sales work has to be fun in order to sustain a career over the long haul. The alternative, dragging the sales aids around, parroting the protocols, is just too grim for the Street-Smart salesman. I'm focused on the human element, on behavior, the interaction of personalities. It's liberating when you can trust yourself to rely on your wits. What's more, such self-reliance delivers you total control over all outcomes. Total? Did I say "total" control? I did. Because, in the

Street-Smart seller's world, there's always another deal and no loss is fatal. *That's* control. If you're not having fun at your sales job, if I have anything to do with it, you soon will be.

In the textbook I used for my teaching, a sales manager is quoted on the subject of how to interview recruits. Many times, he reports, an applicant will be asked to sell the interviewer something right at hand—right on the spot—a pen from the desktop, let's say. "Seven of ten [applicants]," he estimates, fail to do "the one thing he's got to do—*ask for the order*"[1] (emphasis mine). The implication is that the sales manager would not hire anyone who committed this crime. For this reason, I would advise that, during a job interview, you remember to ask for the order on the first meeting. But in the real world, I advise you to defy your customers' expectations at every turn. Get them to close *you*.

■ ■ ■

How do you get a customer to open up to you, you ask? By *surprising* her. For instruction, I refer you to reruns of Peter Falk's *Columbo* TV series. The rumpled lieutenant, ever underestimated by his fellow police officers and the murderer of the week, masks his razor-sharp eye for detail with shabby clothes and a lot of mumbling and fumbling and head scratching. In every episode, the perpetrator is cocksure he has nothing to fear from this bumbler and, thus disarmed, gives himself away. That rumpled lieutenant is my hero! I have my own personal style, of course, tending toward Italian suits, but my affinity with the lieutenant is otherwise total. "Just one more thing . . . !" I love that! Of course, you've got to do your homework for that gambit to pay off.

Instead of insisting to a restaurant owner that your company's drinking glasses are superior to all others in every way, "Dare to be naive," as the engineer/philosopher Buckminster Fuller advised.[2] Ask her instead, "Why do you want new drinking glasses? These look great!" She will not believe her ears; what you have said is not what any buying professional expects to hear. Every other salesperson who ever darkened her door was on an obvious beeline to the company wallet and insisted that his company's products were the best in the field, at the price, and so on.

What makes a product "the best" anyway? "Best" is a concept that lives in the mind of a customer; it's not a measurable, objective quality. "Best" can mean "cheap" to one prospect, "durable" to another, "beautiful," "unusual," "expensive," and so on. Every answer suggests possible selling strategies. But you can't know which angle to work if you're doing all the talking and, furthermore, if you insist that your products are the best, you will be playing to a stereotype. So pull a Costanza: Do the opposite! Listen. Let the customer talk, and keep her talking. You know that by now. Capitalize upon her surprise, even delight, in finding herself engaged in a reality-based conversation with a salesperson. Now that you have become her confidante, she'll tell you *exactly* why she needs—or desires—new drinking glasses. Need converts to desire pretty easily if comprehension and a little compassion (both supplied by you) are in the mix.

Every time you defy a customer's expectations of a salesperson's behavior, you change the dynamic of the selling scenario in the best possible way. Once a customer feels she doesn't have to worry that you're one of those reps who'll say or do anything to make a sale, you have a value to her that goes beyond price and quality into abstraction, into a comfort zone where the customer feels taken care of, well-understood, and well-represented. Value itself is an abstraction: an opinion, an assessment, an aspiration, a judgment. If, as a salesperson, I can get into your head, if the deals I offer demonstrate my understanding of the particular problems you face and goals you have, then I will earn your trust, the holy grail of selling. Trust, you see, is offered from the heart, not the head, and from the heart it's a very short distance to the wallet.

Just recently, I was at a business luncheon with a prospect and his manager. The pair spent the first half hour putting me on the defensive. "How are you going to do this? That?" Everything they said was confrontational and pessimistic. I responded by putting my hands over my eyes and saying, "I totally believe in what I'm suggesting to you, but I can see that we are not a good fit. You really should go it alone. You have the access and expertise . . . ." And so on.

Silence. Then, for the next hour, they worked equally hard, if not harder, to convince me that we would be a great fit! Any time I resisted, they poured it on, until we came to a deal. People want what they can't have. So, withhold the candy sometimes.

The Street-Smart seller understands, you see, that what he's selling primarily is himself. Your products are likely not very different from those of your competitors. The difference is *you*. It should go without saying that a high-performance salesperson must deliver everything as promised, on time, and for the agreed cost. Obligations must be honored in every detail. Every time you deliver on a great deal as promised, you dispel another lingering, knee-jerk suspicion that customers harbor about salespeople. Every time you e-mail a client a newspaper story of value to him but not, apparently, to you, his satisfaction—with both of you—grows in lockstep with your rising profit margin.

■ ■ ■

Do another opposite: Never overpromise! Overpromising is an insanely (to my way of thinking) popular way to drive and supposedly sweeten an initial sale, but the costs of delivering on overpromises cannot be sustained long-term, so don't even start! Likewise, I advise you to turn your back on the so-called "underpromise and overdeliver" strategy. I can't understand the enduring appeal of this gambit for salespeople, though I know they treasure it for the wiggle room it provides. To me, it's a fundamentally destabilized arrangement, rife with uncertainty, that sets up the customer to be disappointed on those inevitable occasions when an overdelivery isn't possible. That's a hug without a kiss, a disappointment you don't forget. So make your irresistible deals based on solid, sustainable numbers and deliver on time, and as ordered. Let the *occasional* overdelivery be something your customer has reason to hope for (there's the H-word again), but doesn't *expect*. Let your customer do the hoping!

Trust that the customer who is allowed to talk about her problems and aspirations will take you where you need to go. When you push a product line hard, running a company script, the customer's guard goes up and stays up, sometimes for good. But if you do the opposite and maintain a considerate distance while asking nonthreatening questions that prove you're listening, the customer will come closer. Few people are quick to give up the great feeling of being the center of attention, and this restaurant owner has to buy drinking glasses from somebody, right? Now, because of your relaxed manner and the respectful curiosity you've shown, she's inclined to trust you. Once a customer makes an emotional commitment to a sales professional, she is yours until someone comes up with a better value proposition—a possibility your reality-based relationship will render remote.

Let's say you're selling BMWs and a guy drives onto the lot in a two-year-old Acura, a status car by any standard. The conventional playbook would call for you to greet this prospect with something along the lines of, "How can I help you today?" or "What brings you to BMW today?" The Street-Smart seller *defies* a prospect's expectations, remember, so do the opposite! Opposites attract. *Compliment* the stranger on his Acura, praise the brand in some detail (it pays to know your competition, too). *Then* ask what brings "the owner of a very nice Acura" to your showroom today.

The prospect's defenses will now be in full retreat because you recognized and treated him as a gentleman of distinction who understands fine automobiles. Now he will feel comfortable divulging to you some of the short-comings he's experienced with the Acura. Remember, no one brags about what a great thing (car, house, watch, book, barbecue, anything) they were *sold*. People brag about what they *bought* based on their own good taste and enviable ability to bargain. Help your customer to see you as a person of distinction in your own right by qui-etly acknowledging his own. We don't do business with statistics—we make deals with living, breathing people, one at a time.

Defiance of expectations not only makes a favorable impression on your customers; your colleagues and your competition will notice it, too. During the 1990s, when I was the top salesperson in New York City in my field, I was not only creating value for my customers by upending everything they thought they knew about salesmen, I was also intimidating the other sales reps, those working for my own company as well as those working for the competition. If I saw a gaggle of sales reps huddled together talking shop or otherwise wasting time, I never broke stride. I knew you don't make money jawing over lunch with other sales reps; it's far more productive to take a *prospect* to lunch and talk about *his* problems! The other reps knew that I was after their meal money, too. There surely were a lot of unkind things thought and said about me, but I never cared—my focus and drive was that intense. Besides, I was having good-paying fun turning their customers into my gold. I didn't experience my lack of camaraderie with lower performing sales reps as a loss or any other kind of problem. The attention I paid my clients paid off in a way I could understand: dollars and cents. I could never say the same for water cooler small talk.

Years later, I came to supervise many of the people I would not give the time of day to back in the trenches. They all said the same thing about me in this new circumstance: That it's fun to work for me and they hope they don't ever have to compete against me again.

To them and to you I say, "Of course, it's fun to work for me—I'm always trying to at least have a little fun!"

The Street-Smart Seven!

- Do the opposite! It can be very productive to try things differently.

- For sales work to be fun, focus on the human element, not just the numbers.

- Each time you defy a customer's expectations you shift the dynamic of the selling cycle in the best possible way.

- Earn trust by offering ideas and deals that demonstrate your understanding of a problem voiced by your customer. Trust is the holy grail of premium sales!

- Understand that ultimately what you're selling is yourself. Your products are likely not very different from those of your competitors. The difference is *you*.

- Never overpromise! The long-term costs of delivering on overpromises are not sustainable, so don't set the precedent.

- Forego the so-called "underpromise and overdeliver" strategy, no matter how much wiggle room it temporarily provides. It's a fundamentally destabilized arrangement that can only end in disappointment on those inevitable occasions when overdelivery isn't possible.

17

Getting to the Truth: Asking Effective Questions

Everyone is ignorant, only on different subjects.
—Will Rogers

Since, in defiance of conventional selling wisdom, you're only going to be talking from 20 to 30 percent of the time, you have to make your every word count. You're going to accomplish this by asking probing but always indirect questions of your customer—questions sufficient to keep him talking and revealing the kinds of information you need to lasso him. Your humble questions and genuine curiosity should cast your customer into the role of instant guru, a person of experience and authority. Everyone welcomes that kind of validation.

Asking oblique but sincere questions not only builds trust and yields relevant information; it also shortens the overall length of the selling cycle. The sooner you put a customer's initial lie-to-the-salesman phase behind you, the closer you'll be to a deal. And the sooner you bring one deal to a conclusion, the sooner you can turn your attention to the next customer—and the next deal.

Here's my Number 1 Rule for opening up a conversation with a client: *Level the playing field.* Get on a first-name basis on day one. When I introduce myself to anyone, I say, "Pleased to meet you. I'm Anthony," not, "Anthony Belli, Acme Company." Invariably, any professional so addressed will answer with his or her first name, feeling, correctly, that it would be rude, even snobbish, to do otherwise. First names put us on equal footing, acknowledging each other's status as professionals. Equal footing makes conversation flow more easily. First dates call for first names.

Rule Number 2: Never ask questions that can only generate a "yes" or "no" answer. "Yes" and "No" are conversation concluders, the opposite of what you want with a prospect, which is to keep the conversation going. Knowledge is power, and useful information can be elicited from stray comments, from thoughts spoken out loud. You won't hear any of that good stuff unless you give the customer both a relevant topic and a soapbox.

What is an indirect question? Indirect questions tend to be longer than direct questions ("Would you mind telling me where you were?" versus "Where were you?") and they often rephrase something that's just been said. They're gentle. Think about it this way. Which question would you be more likely to answer: "How much money did you make last year?" or "What kind of compensation do people in your industry earn?" Which of these two questions is likely to generate a serious answer: "Are you kidding?" or "Do you foresee any problems with that approach?" As time goes on, a customer will reward your deference with more and more expansiveness precisely because you make him feel comfortable and authoritative in a situation he's not accustomed to enjoying.

Phrase your questions so your customer can decide how revealing he wants to be in his response. You have to appreciate that people can be very wary of what their answers might reveal about them, both personally and professionally. Put your customer in the driver's seat, not the hot seat. The hot seat is only for rare and special occasions, like when a customer can't make a decision, a situation we'll talk about shortly. In East Harlem, much success was had with the negatively phrased questions that give the questioned an opportunity to come around to the inviolable opposite, a *yes*. Questions like, "I don't suppose you would be able to watch my Tommy for an

hour or so . . . ?" Or, "I don't suppose I could borrow your
_____?" It works.

It's also true that sometimes people haven't thought
enough about the subject of your inquiry to be able to
give you an honest answer—probably no salesperson has
ever asked these kinds of questions before! Recognize
when this happens and acknowledge it to the customer;
don't let a client feel like she doesn't know something
important. You want her to enjoy her time in the driver's
seat, so let her off the hook. If she hesitates, suggest that
it may have been too soon or otherwise not the right
time for you to ask that particular question. Everyone
appreciates a dignified way out. More important, she'll
have an answer for you next time, whether or not you ask
again! That's when you'll know for sure, not just because
I told you so, that it is possible to get deep enough into a
client's head that she wants to *please* you.

Keep in mind that all people believe their problems
are different from everyone else's, so let your customers
know that you want to understand their concerns specifically. It's amazing how many points you can score with
a client by using modest, Columbo-like phrases like,
"Could you please repeat that?"

Certainly, you should readily admit to what you don't
know or can't follow. But you can *pretend not to follow*,
again, just as Columbo did, in order to communicate your
intention to understand the stresses weighing upon your
customer. You're not revealing yourself to be an idiot by
saying, "I'm sorry, I don't follow"; you're extending your

customer's time in the driver's seat. If I can play dumb—I, who once believed with total certainty that I really *was* dumb—then you can affect a momentarily baffled posture and still be at peace with yourself. Customers, I assure you, can tell the difference between stupidity and curiosity. Be brave—learn to play dumb!

Once, in answer to your nonthreatening questions, a client begins to outline his issues and aspirations, it becomes your job to validate their importance. Again, proceed gently, but pointedly. Ask, "What have you done to address this issue?" "That sounds like it could have worked. What could have gone wrong?" "Is there a limit to the time/money you have to fix this problem?" and so on. Because they encourage a customer to project into the future, "What if?" questions can elicit particularly useful information; open-ended questions help your customers define real issues out loud, sometimes for the first time, and reveal problems you can solve. Remember: Customers don't turn away from real solutions to real problems. They can't afford to!

The Street-Smart Seven!

- Level the playing field. Get on a first-name basis with your customer right from the start.
- Ask sincere but indirect, nonthreatening questions about your customer's particular circumstances.

- Don't ask questions with only "Yes" or "No" answers unless you're sure of the answer and it's the answer you want.

- Play dumb to elicit new information. Nothing sparks an unguarded comment like a dose of dead air.

- Things said to dispel silence are usually ill-considered and may well reveal exploitable information.

- Your questions should put the prospect in the driver's seat, not the hot seat.

- Don't solve your customer's problems too quickly. Instead, make your deals worth a customer's wait.

18

The Will to Walk: Negotiating

Character may almost be called the most effective means of persuasion.

—Aristotle

All sales trainers teach, in this matter correctly, that the upper hand in a negotiation is strong in direct proportion to the willingness, or perceived willingness, both yours and your customer's, to walk away from the table. Of course, no sales trainer really wants you to walk away or get into a contest to see who will walk away first. But I have defied conventional wisdom and walked away plenty of times. Because my confidence is high, my business strong and prospects ever-bright, even before I get into a negotiation I know exactly where my price point is and how I am willing to negotiate my terms (for instance, the payment schedule) in order to get it. And I stick to it. I set my number as high above the midpoint as I deem achievable under the circumstances.

Making a habit of "splitting the difference" will not make you rich. The phrase is widely interpreted to indicate an honorable intention, a dispassionate removal of a final obstacle. Personally, I find it's too often done reflexively, without due consideration, certainly without due calculation. A Street-Smart salesman must *unlearn the impulse to split the difference*. You go to great lengths to demonstrate yourself to be a cut above, so make your numbers a cut above, too. Why undermine your authority at a critical moment in a negotiation by lowering the price? Are you worth the premium to this customer or not? Be consistent throughout the selling cycle; don't allow anxiety to get the better of you. If a customer is going to be demanding of your time, he has to pay for it. Otherwise, he's costing you money in the form of time you could be spending pursuing other business.

I touched on this before in our discussion of pitching to a committee, but in setting prices, never, ever suggest to a client that he is being gouged by the competition. Such insinuations make a customer suspicious of all parties, you included, when your primary task is to set yourself apart. Remember, you don't compare to the other guy in any way; ignore him. Structure your deal based only on what you know about the client's needs, circumstance, aspirations, and your bottom line; forget about the competition.

If you have been following my advice and eliciting all manner of relevant information in creative, confidence-building ways, you will have more power in the negotiations than most sales reps ever have or even imagine they could have. Most sales reps are following rubrics based on averages and generalities, with freebies for kindling and small talk for filler. You, on the other hand, are working a plan based on information specific to your customer, his personality and circumstances.

Any time you proffer a deal that favors, or even appears to favor a client's interests over your own, you set a bad precedent with that customer, a precedent that's almost impossible to overcome in future deals. It's hard to earn your way to premium prices with overpampered customers; in point of fact, it's uphill all the way. Too few salespeople realize this; they think their profit margin with a client will inevitably rise with each transaction. They're wrong. Once you allow a customer to bully you, he'll expect to beat you up the next time, too. That's why he's chosen to do business with you, sucker!

Ultimately, you want to be in a position to get rid of unprofitable, time-wasting customers. If a customer is always complaining, always asking for valuable giveaways, do the math. Tally up the real cost of your time and energy: How much money is draining from your pocket while you

listen to his whining and scheming? Let the worst offend-
ers drift away. Let them waste your competition's time
instead, leaving your rivals with less time to needle your
good customers. The one and only exception to this rule is
when an enervating customer regularly recommends you
to colleagues in ways that pay off in dollars and cents. Only
then is it worthwhile to put up with his grumbling.

Even then, there is the Street-Smart way to handle
such pesky customers. I tell them that it has become
apparent that I, the seller, am not living up to the customer's expectations and suggest that maybe we are a bad
fit. Generally, a customer will be better behaved after
hearing this kind of "push-away." Not forever changed,
but brought to heel for the time being.

The fear of losing a deal drives too many salespeople
to leave money on the table. Nobody wins all the time,
not you, me, Mariano Rivera, or Muhammad Ali. What
distinguishes the greatest players is their takeaway, what
they learn from their efforts, win or lose. They scrutinize
their own game plan and performance, as well as their
opponent's, looking for exploitable patterns and weak
elements. As they identify vulnerabilities, they look for
ways to minimize them. They change their workout
routine, adjust their timing, the angle of their swing.
The goal is always to be a better player the next time
out, to show an opponent (who will also have done his
homework) something he's never seen before.

You can be great—or greater—at selling, too, if
you're genuinely unafraid of the occasional loss. That's

why you have a pipeline full of prospects, right? That's why you visualize every aspect of the selling cycle, why you are a gracious listener who asks only nonthreatening questions to gain exploitable information, isn't it? All that work has been done to allay your anxiety, to provide you with good reason to believe that if this deal doesn't work out, the next one will. There are times when you introduce yourself to a prospect and know right off that the chemistry is not there. Maybe you bear some physical resemblance to someone she dislikes. Let her go. Take the hit and move on.

That's because "like" helps, "neutral" is fine, but "dislike" is a real challenge, because dislike functions like earmuffs. It muffles your voice, making it difficult for the customer to hear what you have to say, to perceive your value equation. If you can't overcome it quickly, you will have to move on.

Uncertainty is costly in a charged situation like a negotiation. It is best eliminated and you can learn to do it. Late-inning concessions (such as reflexively splitting the difference) arise from self-doubt like smoke from fire and fill the room just as quickly. If you find yourself giving in to anxiety during a negotiation, resolve to be better prepared the next time no matter what happens today. Meanwhile, stick to the bottom line you set for yourself in the deal at hand *whether or not* it leads to a sale.

Anxious sellers also too often convince themselves that the other rep has more and better resources at his disposal; they worry they will be outmaneuvered.

Usually this is an upfront worry, but a lot of reps cite the competition's bells and whistles after they lose a deal, too. In the long run, giving in, giving voice, to this kind of worry is no more than a self-defeating attempt to justify future failures or dodge the blame for a past one. Don't fall into this habit.

As a matter of fact, I want you to ignore any talk or mention of the competition in the presence of your clients. Customers can be expected to try at least to exploit a salesperson's anxiety by pitting vendor against vendor. It's often the best gambit they think they have, poor things. Be dismissive of their clumsily veiled threats. Remind such a scheming customer that your offers are based on two things: (1) your products, and (2) on facts specific to the customer's circumstance. Add that you trust him to make the right choice for his business when the moment comes.

This is another good time, then, to do the opposite. When a customer blasts your competitor, respond by saying, "Overall, I hear that they're pretty great to do business with." Invariably, the customer will now tell you more ways in which he specifically dislikes your competition. This is premium exploitable information!

Should you believe a customer who tells you he can get the same thing from another vendor for several percent less? The answer is sometimes. But *which* times, you ask? Again, if you've been letting your customer do most of the talking, you have a pretty extensive mental dossier on him by now. You almost certainly know what motivates him far better than your vaunted competition does. This is the moment to access your inner poker player; it can be useful to do a little reading on the way high-stakes poker players spot their opponents' "tells," the small, unconscious behaviors that betray big truths like "I didn't draw to the full house." Do your customer's statements and body language add up? Has his behavior changed significantly since the last time you spoke or saw each other? Weigh words against behavior—posture, tone of voice—to make your best assessment of his truthfulness. Did he look you in the eye when he spoke of the large discount the competition supposedly offered? It's a rare bird that can look right at you and lie, though they do exist. Sometimes people shake their head from left to right, as in "No," when they're saying the word "Yes." Red flag! You'll be amazed and enriched by the valuable information you'll find right in front of you if you take the time to look.

Make sure your words and actions are in alignment, too. If you're really interested and open to what your customer has to say, you won't be sweating. Examine your unconscious behaviors with a magnifying glass. Unlearn them! Present your customer with the same consistency in words and appearance that would encourage you to believe what she has to say.

With practice, believe me, you'll become confident in your ability to assess whether a customer is bluffing. If he's just nervous and talking trash, you'll learn to spot that, too. The thing so few sellers realize is that customers are almost never completely intractable once they've gone some distance with you. Pretty much the last thing an overcautious buyer wants to do is repeat the process all over again with another rep. That's another reason why it's so important for you to distinguish yourself, to give a customer good reason to leave his long-time relationship.

Trust the information you've been gathering about this client and his business. The other rep is no doubt following standard procedure, pushing a hard sell and doing his frantic best to keep the customer from getting a word in edgewise. By contrast, you've formed a problem-solving alliance that protects you from empty threats like another 10 percent off from the other guy.

A Street-Smart Eight!

- Any deal favoring the client's interests over your own sets a bad, almost insurmountable precedent. Once you allow a customer to bully you, he'll expect to beat you up next time too, sucker!

- When setting prices, resist the temptation to low-ball. "Splitting the difference" will not make you rich. You are a cut above average; your prices should be too.

- Know your price point *before* entering a negotiation. Stick to it and use terms to get it.

(continued)

(continued)

- Never suggest that a customer is being gouged by the competition. It makes a customer suspicious of everybody, including you.

- Don't play into customers' attempts to kindle a price war between you and the competition. Remind scheming customers that your offers are based on your products and facts specific to the customer's circumstance. Let him know you trust him to make the right choice for his business when the moment comes.

- School a whining, demanding customer by suggesting that the two of you might be a bad fit. If his behavior doesn't improve, let him waste your competitors' time.

- Make sure your words and actions are aligned. Examine your unconscious behaviors (what poker players call "tells") with a magnifying glass—then unlearn them!

- The fear of losing a deal causes too many salespeople to leave money on the table. What distinguishes the greatest players is their takeaway, what they learn from their efforts, win or lose. Be prepared to walk away. Generally, the last thing a customer wants is to repeat the whole process with another rep!

CHAPTER

19

Flag on the Play!
Reading a Customer

You can observe a lot just by watching.

—Yogi Berra

A few years ago, I drove four hours in one direction to accompany a new rep in her first face-to-face meeting with a big-fish prospect. I wanted to see my rookie in action. She was feeling confident, certain her potential customer was hyper–price-conscious and equally certain that if she were aggressive in her pricing, we would land the account. Aggressive pricing was the only candy she was holding—not much of a game plan in the city

183

playgrounds of my youth. I've lived long enough to know that when a customer says, "It's all about price," he's lying, plain and simple. "It" is never all about price; people are too multidimensional for that to be the case. If a self-described price-conscious customer is, furthermore, also unwilling to share any information with you about his business, as this one was, he is not ready to do business. In any event, I never head into a meeting in which my supposed strength is my willingness to take less money than I want.

Salespeople tend to think of undercutting the competition on price as a fifth ace, an almost surefire way of getting to "Yes." I know otherwise because I have my own surefire ways of getting to "Yes." I also know that it's easier to accurately remember what *happened* than to accurately remember what you were *told*, so I make it a habit to let my reps learn for themselves, that price is the weakest of sales differentiators. I always ask my reps, after an aggressive pricing strategy leaves them with a completed sale but an overall loss, "Did you think the client was going to ask you how he could pay more for your product?" They are usually forced to confess—and surprised to realize—they hadn't given the idea of *raising* their prices any thought at all! Yet premium pricing is the hallmark of a high-performance salesperson. The Street-Smart seller's mandate is to build his case for those higher prices.

Recently, on a stroll through Central Park in New York, I saw a crowd gathered to watch a bunch of poor, shabbily dressed kids break-dancing. They'd already engaged the audience with a few really good moves; by the time I arrived, they were talking up the big finale. They picked six people from the crowd and lined them up. One of the dancers announced that he was going to jump over all six at one time—with a mid-air somersault for good measure. Then he added that he knew if he did the trick without collecting money first, everyone would leave without paying. He didn't have an attitude about it; it was just a fact and drew a laugh from the crowd. I knew they'd learned that lesson the hard way, the only way information comes to kids like these. "So we're gonna pass the hat *now*!" he shouted, and the group spent several minutes hitting up the assembled for their pocket change and talking up the trick like carnival barkers: Could he really do it, jump *and* flip? I threw in a fin.

When they were satisfied they'd extracted as much money from the onlookers as possible, the break-dancer did the trick to perfection, exactly as promised. And sure enough, the crowd dispersed, paid-up and guilt-free! These street kids understood what I'm trying to impart to you: the cardinal rule of Street-Smart selling: Never hand over the candy until you are compensated! *Never* undersell yourself.

So, despite my rep's weak hand, I made the drive so that I could further school her in the Street-Smart selling approach I employ with such success. Within minutes of sitting down with the prospect in his office, I knew we had a better chance of replacing Derek Jeter in the Yankee line-up than of getting this man's business. Why? Because three red flags went up in succession, each missed or ignored by my rep in turn.

For starters, Mr. Prospect began the meeting by letting us know what a fair and ethical guy he is. Flag! All the major con men in East Harlem did this. Dealers will assure junkies of the superior quality of their dope versus the other guy's, as if the junkie's health was the foremost thing on his mind. And the junkies believe them because they are desperate. But believe this: People who go out of their way to let you know how trustworthy they are cannot be trusted. It's as simple as that. Truly good people communicate by example; they don't blow their own horns. So right away, I knew the guy was not going to be honest in his dealings. I also knew that whatever he'd said to my rep to make her think price was all that mattered was almost surely bogus.

Minutes later he asked me, in front of my rep but as if we were alone, if I knew what would happen to his current sales rep, the guy from our competition, if our two companies merged under my company's logo, as was then under negotiation. I considered the possibility that his concern was intended only to further convince me of his status as a truly good guy—you know, like when a person insists he "doesn't see color." That's the way my mind works.

"He's a great guy and I'd hate to lose him," Mr. Prospect went on. It was possible that his concern for his longtime vendor might be real, but his vaunted compassion obviously didn't extend to my sales rep, who was by now genuinely uncomfortable. I replied that his was an interesting question for which I had no definite answer, and he accepted my answer because it was obviously true—the merger was still under discussion. But now I knew for sure that price was never going to be enough of a motivator to get this guy to sever a valued relationship. In fact, in all likelihood, our company's price simply was being used to get a better price from the existing vendor—might I add, from the "great guy" he supposedly cares for?

Third, when I asked, after my rep's roll-out of several aggressive pricing options, if we could take him to lunch, he declined, asserting that he "never goes out" with vendors because it's "just inappropriate." Really? Then how did he build such a strong relationship with another sales rep that he's worried about the guy losing his job? I didn't ride for four hours for a lecture on ethics by the likes of this guy. Now I was certain there was no money to be made here.

My rep had completely misread the situation and what she did wrong is what most sales reps do wrong. They prefer to believe that there's a deal, some deal, to be made, even if it's not the best deal, and then they squander precious resources (this expedition cost a full day off both our calendars) chasing a phantom. This customer was not long-term material; he was already in a committed relationship! But my rookie never got a read on him because she hadn't put in the time to get into his head, to plant the idea that he'd do well to work with her, with us. She'd been doing all the talking, just as she'd been taught, focused like a laser on price and performance and parroting our company's sales script, the one I ignore. This guy wasn't worth a phone call, much less an eight-hour drive. She'd been playing by the tired old sales book, hoping she could win in the end by undercutting the other guy. Another salesperson undone by that old demon, Hope. All sales relationships can be broken, and if my rep had made her way first into the heart and mind of this customer instead of focusing on his wallet, she might have won him over. But she wasn't Street-Smart enough to make it happen.

There are times when you should walk away from a prospect and this was one of them. The guy was raising red flags with every other sentence. No doubt he was also feeling puffed up about how far we'd driven to meet with him; he probably teases and milks the competition's reps, too. My rep had expended significant time and thought calculating lowball offers that Mr. Prospect at most would use against another rep—if he didn't toss them directly into the circular file. She didn't understand that cutting this prospect loose wouldn't be walking away from something, it would be walking *toward* something else!

Some old habits die hard, even though they're killable. You know what my rep said to me at lunch afterward, even as I explained how I understood what had happened? She said, "I know you don't think we have a shot with this guy, but he will bite on the low price. You'll see." No sooner were the words out of her mouth than Mr. Ethics walked into the restaurant with a competing salesman.

Which brings me to the subject of dealing with dislikable people, a common enough circumstance. When someone strikes you as a real jerk, find something to focus on in him that inspires a feeling other than revulsion. Disdain tells, and it makes a premium price deal all but impossible. You've got to level the playing field so you can deal with this person, so excuse his behaviors while considering how you might exploit them. Ignore slights, stupid comments; move past them. The ability to forget is every bit as important as the ability to remember because it enables you to reshuffle the deck. Let the things you elect to overlook be a source of equilibrium for you.

Never let a customer's disagreeable qualities throw you off your game. You don't get to choose your land-lord; you just have to deal with him. You don't get to choose the buyer either; you just have to *work* her in order to work *with* her. Even though Mr. Ethics was in a committed relationship, that didn't mean he couldn't be enticed to break it. But my rep must have known about the relationship, and she hadn't put any effort into getting into his head; it had all been strictly a num-bers game. She wasted valuable time and harvested none of the kind of inadvertently revealing personal information that can bring a committed customer to his tipping point, the place where he is open to working with a new vendor.

The Street-Smart Seven!

- Beware price-cutting! Never head into a meeting in which your supposed strength is your willingness to take less money than you want.
- If a supposedly price-conscious customer is unwilling to share any further information about his business, he is not ready to do business. Don't waste your time.
- If an aggressive pricing strategy leaves you with a completed sale but an overall loss, ask yourself, "How did I ever think the client was going to ask me how he could pay more?" Then find that way!
- People who go out of their way to let you know how trustworthy they are cannot be trusted. Truly good people communicate by example, not by blowing their own horns.
- The ability to forget is as important as the ability to remember: When someone strikes you as a real jerk, find something to focus on in him that inspires a feeling other than revulsion. Disdain tells, and makes a premium price deal all but

impossible. Excuse his behaviors while determining how you might exploit them.

- Never hand over the candy until you are compensated! Ever!
- A salesperson who cuts a prospect loose knows he is not walking away from anything, but *toward* something else.

CHAPTER

20

Closing, or The Gentle Kill

Even if you beat me, I'm still the best.
—Fast Eddie, *The Hustler*

A skillful closer has the ability to identify the best time, even the precise moment, to distill all the elements of a negotiation into a clear choice for the customer between "Yes" and "No." All the knowledge you gathered and the insights it yielded, the information that let you customize your offer to this client, now contributes to the Street-Smart seller's ability to identify this critical moment when it comes and to maneuver through it skillfully. In fact, our clients are so juiced for the problem-solving deal we've outlined and the clear benefits of working with a Street-Smart seller, they're more motivated to sign than other customers.

That said, before moving in for the gentle kill—that is, a signature—take a split second to remind yourself that not everything rides on this deal. Street-Smart sellers cultivate the confidence to responsibly rely on an inner calm consistent with their well-founded belief that there will be other opportunities, maybe even with this same customer, no matter what happens right now. Believe me, future-focused confidence makes a tremendously positive impression on customers, and more often than not delivers the winning hand. A person in control of his or her destiny, with a credible willingness to walk away from the proceedings, is almost irresistibly impressive.

It takes real nerve to walk that line; I won't deny it. But the Street-Smart methods that have brought you this far will help you find your nerve, your courage, with an implied capital C. Over the course of history, many great minds have considered the source of courage, but there is surprisingly little agreement among them. Some equate courage with fearlessness, but fearlessness isn't always a good thing; it can lead to recklessness, a behavior that has no place in business. Courage, on the other hand, is always a good and inspiring thing. "Courage," Sir Winston Churchill is said to have said (no one will say where or when), is "going from failure to failure without losing enthusiasm." I wish I'd said it! Whoever said it is exactly right.

In my view, courage is the willingness and ability to take action despite being afraid. It is the capacity to gather your wits, focus, conceive, and carry out a plan in the face of overwhelming odds. For those of us in the sales profession, courage is founded in the confidence that arises from being certain that you will prevail, now or later. I can get my ass kicked day after day and not call it a week. I come to my job without fear because I know that when everyone else backs down—and all salespeople have disappointing weeks—I'll still be standing and ready to strike.

There is never only one way to win. If someone could out-fight me, I'd out-smart him. Or out-hustle him, or out-network him, whatever resource is necessary. With courage, you give yourself options, ways to win. That's the Street-Smart seller's way.

■   ■   ■

Whether or not a sales rep suffers from chronic heartburn generally correlates with how calm he is at the do-or-die moments in the sales cycle. "How do I ask for the business?" is the central question that can bother, cost, undercut, haunt, and even defeat a sales rep over the years. I understand that it's difficult to ask for help, to admit that you need assistance, but to succeed in this trade you're going to have to get over your reticence. If you don't ask, you don't get: It's that simple. Sometimes you don't even get if you ask, and that's too bad, but it doesn't change the fact that the odds of acquiring anything from anybody improve tremendously if preceded by a reasonable request.

It's debilitating to be in a profession that requires you to work toward a situation—the closing—in which the other side invariably has the upper hand. It's crazy-making and I won't do it. Instead, I engineer closings when I arrive at the perception of having addressed and solved the customer's problems. Doing so gives me the authority to decide that the conversation is over and the ability to effectively resist a customer's not-unexpected ruses or threats to go with the competition, and to do so at a percentage that has made me a wealthy man. To turn the tables this way, you need to trust the Street-Smart seller's instincts that you're now always fine-tuning.

I hope you weren't thinking I was going to teach you how to spot some telltale facial tic or posture that betrays a customer's vulnerability to your request for a signature. Body language is highly communicative, it's true, but lots of people are good at reading it, even some customers. What sets Street-Smart sellers apart is that when the time comes to put pen to paper, they *recognize the moment* because the moment is *theirs* to identify, not the customer's. The offer has been put into writing exactly as discussed; there's nothing further to explain. Remember: If you can cure his pain, he will want to close you!

What the customer needs to understand from this identified moment forward is that if she or he doesn't seal the deal now, you're taking your marbles and moving on to another, smarter customer. The price isn't going to go any lower and you have another appointment. Let the customer worry that he's missing out on a great deal that the others on your crowded dance card are enjoying. Work the universally shared dislike of being left out in the cold to your advantage. No one likes to feel left out of a cool club, not hoodlums or altar boys or company procurement officers.

In a heightened state of anxiety perhaps bordering on panic, the typical sales rep runs memorized scenarios through her mind at a closing, rifling through the standard playbook at warp speed. Do I do the "Trial" close? Do I run the "These Are Your Options" close? Such scripts are the only choices she thinks she has, and they are all predatory gimmicks of the same familiar and totally dislikable vulture. Underlying her desperate calculations is the fear that she could miss her chance with this customer by choosing the wrong gambit. The moment a customer senses her insecurity he will become resistant, betting that a price cut will be the result. Prove that customer wrong!

You, the Street-Smart seller, have learned enough about your customer and his professional goals to know that the offer at hand is tailor-made to solve one or more of his current or ongoing issues. This is all the incentive your customer needs to sign on the dotted line. Your one-time offer is also better than anything he's seen or is going to see from the competition because it comes with *you*, his understanding advocate, into the bargain. You're not like everybody else and all your other customers know it. If this one's not smart enough to figure it out, or too scared to make a move, leave him scratching his head.

Do it my way and you'll never suffer salesman's heartburn again.

■   ■   ■

Before you arrive at a closing, know exactly what you want the customer to do and how you're going to communicate your expectation, a ripe subject for visualization. Know what you want; see the setting, set conversations in motion. No matter how well you know him, keep running the scenario until you're satisfied you've got a way to talk to the client that doesn't make either of you nervous or uncomfortable. Take that attitude with you to the closing.

Always be clear about the "ask" and never give a customer more than one option to choose from *other than payment terms*. To suggest more than one option is the single worst play to make at closing time and it is, to my way of thinking, shockingly commonplace. Any time you present a customer with multiple options, you're signaling a willingness to completely restart the sales cycle. Did you realize that? You're providing her with a renewed chance to fixate on some, possibly irrelevant, detail she can use to milk you for a sweeter deal. Why would you want to go back to square one this late in the game?

Here's what a Street-Smart seller knows for sure at closing time: I've listened carefully to my customer's concerns and aspirations, provided samples of particular products based on real needs, and ample time to test them in the workplace. I've made a contract offer based on all of the above and the customer has had time to read it with a magnifying glass while considering my terms. Now is the time for a signature.

It's also time for one more game-changer. Now that you have your ducks in a row, offer written out, contract in hand, bottom line intact, delivery assured, *don't* whip out your fountain pen. Instead, ask your customer, "What is our next step?"

I can hear you now. You're saying, "I thought you told me to let the customer know that there are no more options; take it or leave it, I've got another appointment." And again I say unto you, you are only ceding *apparent* control of the situation to your customer. Street-Smart sellers adopt this inquiring stance because we understand that deals move more quickly toward conclusion when the buyer thinks he's in the driver's seat. Your customer is habituated to dread the hard close, the pressure of being in the crosshairs of a hungry sales rep, and surely itching to make a getaway. So surprise him—do the opposite! Ask him what comes next.

If the customer's suggestion for the next step meets with your approval, accept his signature slowly and graciously. If it doesn't, pose this follow-up question: "Why do you see _____ as the next step?" Insert the customer's exact phrasing into the blank space; put him on the defensive without provoking him. You're asking a reasonable question; let him come up with a reasonable answer. Hold your ground. Ideally, you want to have this customer for years, you will be his anointed problem-solver for life. So have faith in the progress of the next few minutes.

Let the customer speak. But remember that closings are different from openings in one very significant way—*because closings happen when there's nothing left to say.* You're not willing to make any less money on this transaction than has been discussed and previously agreed. Take in whatever the customer says but *have no thought of addressing anything other than slight modifications to the contract at hand. Never* offer to recalculate terms at closing time. It's a move that stinks of desperation and spells certain death for any mutually rewarding long-term relationship, even if you get a signature today. It reinforces the idea that you can be made to buckle. Buckle once, and they will try to get you to buckle again the next time. Instead, acknowledge that the deal is over and start packing up. You heard me.

But while you're getting ready to leave, ask, just as Lieutenant Columbo used to ask, just as a point of information, where the deal went wrong. If the customer responds to your inquiry, congratulations! You've entered a new negotiation at the customer's bidding. Keep the focus intense now. Concede again the failure of today's deal while musing upon ways in which the customer's concerns might be addressed in the future. Let the customer feel understood; it's a good feeling and, because she's had this feeling with you before, it reminds her why she wanted to do business with you in the first place: because you're not like other sales reps.

Let me quote the poker-playing playwright David Mamet again, this time at some length, because he makes a very important "big picture" observation highly relevant to the Street-Smart seller, particularly at closing time. "The point is not to win the most hands, the point is not even to win in the most games. The point is to *win the most money* (italics his). This probably means playing less hands than the guy who has just come for the action; it means not giving your fellow players a break because you value their feelings; it means not giving some back at the end of the night because you feel embarrassed by winning; it means taking those steps and creating those habits of thought and action which, in the long run, *must prevail*" (italics mine).[1]

Street-Smart tactics exactly. You have other opportunities to pursue. This customer's time to take advantage of your unbeatable offer is about to expire. Let him know it. There comes a point when a customer is not worth further effort, and it comes sooner than the conventional wisdom would have you think. Have, or pretend to have, the courage to move on to the next customer. Your boldness will pay off over the long run.

Believe it or not, even if today's events come to naught, don't be surprised if you hear from this customer again without any prompting. Customers are not used to having a sales rep pocket the marbles and take the game around the corner. It makes them rub their eyes and shake their heads; such behavior is not easy either to put into context or to dismiss. Thinking back on what happened, they often begin to worry that they missed out on something their competition knows about. It's evident that you're a high-performance professional, so what is it your other clients are paying premium for?

People with power—money, name, access, prestige—are, overwhelmingly, all covetous. They are forever comparing houses and bank accounts, whether they talk about it out loud or not. And in any particular field, they will all have about the same amount of money and stuff. Therefore, when all your competitors' products are pretty much as good as yours and pretty much the same price, *value* is the coin of the realm, not price, and value resides in the mind of the customer. Once I've figured out that you, my customer, have a vision of yourself as a national figure, I'll make it my business to help you get there because vision fulfillment trumps price-cutting every time.

The taking-my-business-elsewhere pendulum swings both ways. Not only can the customer choose to buy from another vendor, you can choose to make great deals *with your customer's competition!* The willingness to let a deal go strongly implies to a customer that others are ready to sign. Let your customer worry that that's what you're up to. Nobody likes to think the other guy is getting a better deal—especially the deal you just turned down. It eats at people.

If curiosity or greed or whatever gets the better of her, and she does decide to take her business elsewhere this time, an abortive customer will very often be nagged by a sense of missed opportunity, even loss. This is the proper place for emotions in a buyer-seller relationship—on the *buyer* side! Now she wants a second chance! A haunted, once-reluctant customer will call again, believe me—either under a genuinely new circumstance or a see-through invented pretext. Or she may simply take your next call, which you will delay until you have conceived an offer that fully addresses her previous last-minute doubts. You've captured the customer's imagination because you've set yourself apart.

■ ■ ■

A person like me who grew up with nothing, understands that all parties to a negotiation, no matter their position, are fearful to some extent. The slumlord may want his money, but he also knows how hard it is, legally and emotionally, to evict a family from their home. He also knows that the next tenants aren't likely to have any more money than the current ones and that they could turn out to be destructive, loud, dirty, criminal, and possess any number of undesirable behaviors and associates. So the landlord wants a deal, too, not just you. Rather than fall prey to a customer's insecurities, Street-Smart sellers work a customer's fears to their advantage.

There's more than one way to play a customer on the verge. Try this with a balky buyer: Ask him how he's made signing decisions in the past. Switch his focus from now, when he's unsure, to then, when he signed his name with a fancy fountain pen. Even if he thinks he made a mistake the last time, as he recalls the sale cycle he'll tell himself that that was another sales rep and another company. He doesn't want the problem to be him, you see. No one does. So now he likes you more than ever. You're not pushy; you're a good listener and an obvious professional. The customer has to buy from somebody; he is *in need*. Keep providing him clear ways to differentiate between you and the other rep, the one breathing down his neck. Then he will sign your contract.

Sometimes a customer will accept the signing pen from you and then hesitate. If this happens, take the pen, literally or metaphorically, from the customer's hand. Tell him that you understand he may not be ready to move forward, and remain silent. Let the room fill with dead air. If you can hang on long enough—sometimes just a microsecond more—the customer may take the pen back just to dispel the unbearable tension.

If he does, now it's *your* turn to be hesitant! Am I kidding? Am I really telling you to slow things down, just when the deal is so close to a happy conclusion? Yes, that's what I'm telling you. Continue to defy expectations, to set yourself apart from other salespeople. Ask him if he's *sure* now. If he's says he isn't, reply, "I didn't think you were," and pocket the pen. Go quiet again. If the customer doesn't insist you give him the pen back now, believe me, he was never going to sign or would have called to cancel the deal tomorrow.

But you'll be surprised, even shocked, to discover how often a customer will insist that you give him back the pen. Take something away and human nature begs it back. People covet what they can't have (do not eat of that one tree!) and dismiss things that come easily. Your extravagant reluctance not to let him sign onto a deal he wasn't 100 percent comfortable with now has him convinced beyond a reasonable doubt that you are an honest person with his best interests in mind. And you are; it just so happens that your best interests dovetail!

And you can take further delight in the knowledge that when your customer takes back the pen for the last time and signs his name to the contract, he's doing it because he thinks he's wresting control of the situation from you, just as you've encouraged him to think all along.

■ ■ ■

No matter the outcome of any single closing, the Street-Smart seller operates under the same rules as the poorest of the poor, people who operate on the assumption that a "Yes" is good for today and a "No" is just for now. There is no permanence to either. The poor also deeply appreciate that "Yes" is dependent on continued good performance and that "Yes" converts to "No" far more easily than vice versa. For the Street-Smart seller, there also is no permanence to "Yes" or "No." We use instinct, experience, inquiry, and observation to turn tides in our favor, and these skills, the basis of our professional self-reliance, give us the capacity to trust in another outcome at another time. We don't believe in the last word. We believe in the next round!

The Street-Smart Seven!

- Future-focused confidence makes a tremendously positive impression on customers, and more often than not delivers the winning hand.

- A salesperson with a credible willingness to walk away from the proceedings is almost irresistibly impressive.

- Always be clear about the "ask" and *never give a customer options to choose among other than payment plans*!

(continued)

(continued)

- Closings are different from openings in one very significant way: *closings happen when there's nothing left to say.*

- Engineer closings so that you arrive at the perception of having addressed and solved the customer's problems, giving you the authority to decide the negotiation is over and the ability to resist a customer's late threats to go with the competition.

- Before moving in for the gentle kill—the signature—take a split second to remind yourself that not everything rides on this deal.

- Game-changer: With contract in hand, bottom line intact, delivery assured, *don't* whip out your fountain pen. Instead ask your customer: "What is our next step?"

The Street-Smart Super Seven!

- Never, ever, offer to recalculate at closing. It stinks of desperation and spells certain death for any mutually rewarding long-term relationship, even if you get the signature today. Instead, calmly acknowledge that the deal is over and start packing up. Have, or pretend to have, the courage to move on. Your boldness will pay off over the long run.

- The taking-my-business-elsewhere pendulum swings both ways. Not only can the customer choose to buy from another vendor, you can choose to make great deals *with your customer's competition!* Customers are not used to having a sales rep pocket the marbles and take the game around the corner. It makes them rub their eyes and shake their heads. They worry that they missed out on something their competition knows about. You'll likely hear from them again.

- Try this with a balky buyer: Ask him how he's made signing decisions in the past. Switch his focus from now, when he's unsure, to then, when he signed. What made the difference? Getting him to articulate the difference may well help you close the deal today.

- Sometimes a customer will accept the signing pen and then hesitate. If this happens, take the pen from the customer and go silent. If you can hang on long enough—sometimes just a microsecond more—the customer may take the pen back just to dispel the tension.

- If he does, it's *your* turn to be hesitant! Continue to defy his expectations. Ask him if he's *sure* now.

(continued)

(continued)

If he's says he isn't, reply, "I didn't think you were," and pocket the pen. Go quiet again. If the customer doesn't insist you give him the pen back now, believe me, he was never going to sign or he would have called you tomorrow to cancel.

- Take something away and human nature begs it back. People covet what they can't have.
- Both Yes and No are answers good for today only. The Street-Smart don't believe in the last word. We believe in the next round!

21

Teaching Instincts

Common sense is instinct. Enough of it is genius.
—George Bernard Shaw

After a professional lifetime as a salesman and a sales-force manager, I know what I'm up against in trying to teach what I learned on the streets to people from solid middle-class backgrounds—like you, probably. I appreciate the challenge I face in teaching what may appear to be instincts ("untaught abilities," to pluralize the Scottish philosopher/clockmaker, Alexander Bain), and I sure don't shrink from it. But I don't think what I'm teaching here is instinct so much as ways to gather information. Not all instincts are inborn, genetic; neither do they arise out of received wisdom. Instincts like mine—those I want to teach you—are *made*, fine-tuned through observation, trial and error. It may seem like I'm asking you to develop some kind of magical sixth sense. I'm not. I'm showing you ways to recognize and collect valuable customer-specific information and to give yourself room to operate. You know more than you think you do. You're just not putting your knowledge to the most profitable use because it's been remunerative enough just to go along with the crowd.

When we encourage little children to trust their instincts, we are encouraging them to pay attention to the way things or people make them *feel*, and in that way to access their inborn sense of right and wrong. As our mental capabilities grow we learn how to override our feelings with various logics. The aspiring Street-Smart seller will put some time into getting back in touch with his or her innate sense of what's fair and what's "no fair" (as we said in East Harlem), because feelings have physical manifestations, in you and in your customers. Be alert to them. Keep your mental intelligence in sync with your physical intelligence because the information conduits they provide are equally valuable.

Making more money makes you feel better, doesn't it? So follow the physical clues that lead to that feeling. As I said at the start of this book, I've never forgotten how good it feels to be on the receiving end of some much-needed assistance. Don't you forget it either; it's the Street-Smart seller's secret weapon. He or she is a customer's problem-solver and ally. Not a buddy, not a kindred spirit, but a champion always making things possible and therefore always a welcome presence.

I'm not suggesting you abandon your present ways wholesale. I know you won't! What I am asking is that you try my methods alongside your usual approach for a while and see what comes of it. Go to the initial meeting with a customer without your luggage. What's different about the experience for you, for him? How did the experience make you feel? What's different about the outcomes when you let the customer do most of the talking? Analyze every aspect of these encounters and build on what you learn. Visualize. Try it again. Carry yourself with courage and creativity, not sales aids. Being different makes a difference, I assure you! Accumulate your own wisdom in the same way I did—by doing it my way.

But rest assured there is no way to accumulate experience without the expenditure of time. Find the energy, because energy brings results and it's results that fuel your energy. It's a highly remunerative cycle. However, it's safe to say that most people, however ambitious they think they are, are unwilling to give up even the minimum necessary in order to achieve major financial success, namely their weekends (both days!) and their TV time. These were never issues for me, I'll admit. Coming up I had nothing to *give* up. I appreciate how simultaneously appealing and daunting my style may appear to you. But if you are going to transform yourself into a Street-Smart seller, you'll make some significant sacrifice of leisure time to set a new course for yourself and your business. Otherwise, this has been just an uplifting story and an intellectual exercise. Your ability to master the techniques and tactics I've described will be limited only by the time you give to trial and error. And there will be errors. Errors are committed on any learning curve. Expect them, and do not be intimidated. This is true in any pursuit of achievement. Don't be afraid of failures. They are missteps, not road wrecks.

At age 54, I decided to compete in the 100-meter dash in New York's Empire State Games. Patterned after the Olympics, the state games were the first of their kind in the country and became the standard for multi-sport amateur athletic programs. Now I'd played ball all my life but I was never a track athlete; I didn't know the first thing about sprinting, but I knew there are always more ways than the obvious to win at anything. No sooner did I make the decision to enter the race than I began to realize how afraid I was that I might finish last after a bad stumble at the starter's pistol, or pull a hamstring and have to be removed from the oval on a stretcher with thousands watching.

To allay my fears, I went to see the track coach, Dr. Darryl Bullock, at Mercy College, where I was then on the business faculty. I told him the goal I had set for myself and he agreed to coach me. We met at 6:15 A.M. for several sessions over the next few months. He began my training by asking me to think about my successes in baseball and business and, specifically, the abilities I'd had to cultivate in order to become a high achiever, the ability to relax, to commit, to focus. These types of skills are highly transferable to other endeavors, he assured me, and I knew he was right because my East Harlem street-smarts had translated so well to salesmanship. Only fear could keep me from doing my best out on the track, and our best is all we can ask of ourselves. By the time the day of the race dawned, I was as prepared, physically and psychologically, as I felt I could be. What happened, you ask? I pulled a hamstring *during* the race and still took the bronze! Not only was I not taken from the field on a stretcher, I took home a medal.

Of course, I wanted to build on my success, so I turned my attention to the U.S.A. Track and Field Association (USATF) Eastern Regional summer games, a step up, competitively, from the Empire State Games. I entered the 100-meter dash in my age group. Now I know that consistent effort will deliver consistent rewards, and I also know that to ramp up your game, you can't go it alone, not as an athlete and not as a salesperson. Once you set a higher goal, you have to redouble your efforts and bring every possible resource to bear. I needed someone new on my team and after careful research, I began regular training with Kiyafa, a professional speed coach from Velocity Sports Performance in Westchester, New York. While we can't know exactly how our intensified effort will pay off, we can do our best to ensure that it will and constancy is key. In this instance, with regular training sessions and the support of Kiyafa's experience, wisdom and guidance, I took the *gold*.

▪ ▪ ▪

Early in my freshman year, the African American literature professor I spoke of earlier assigned us to read Ralph Ellison's *Invisible Man*. It was pretty much the first book I'd ever read from cover to cover, and I was completely knocked out by it, by the *accuracy* of it. Ellison knew *exactly* what it was like to count for nothing; I *knew* he knew. Even though he was talking about another part of Harlem, he told a tale I could feel the truth of in my bones, and it helped to foster a real philosophical awakening in me, the understanding that people are far more deeply connected by socio-economic circumstances than by ethnicity. I wish more people understood this! We would have a lot more peaceful and stable society.

Ellison's nameless narrator looks back on a surreally difficult life of institutional and personal anonymity from a hard-earned perspective. At midlife, the forces against him have proven so huge that he now understands he must *embrace his invisibility for the advantages it can provide*. That's exactly what I mean when I say, "Your advantage is that no one takes you seriously." What the Street-Smart seller knows that gives him a fundamental edge is that when people regard you as nothing more than a filler of space, *then unintentionally they give you an opening*, a doorknob that we, the enlightened, jiggle every time.

Let me also remind you that you can—you *have to*—piece things together: business deals, courtships, even dinner. You don't have to have all your ducks in a row before you can make a move. In fact, you can't! Things just don't proceed that way, not in nature, not in your personal life, and not in your professional life. Things happen incrementally, a little at a time. Some things have to be dealt with every day, some every week or year. Some are to be expected and some are not. Actually, so far as I can tell it's only big, unexpected things that happen all at once, though with consequences unfolding over time. There is no time like the present for getting started at anything though, so do not delay. Begin introducing my methods into your selling life one by one, here and there, steadily and over time. Give them their test runs. I predict you will come around to my way of thinking and doing.

I predict this because, as a salesforce manager, I've been like nothing so much as an on-call psychotherapist. I believe I've heard it all. In this sluggish economy especially, reps call me day and night to report yet another price-cut deal they made because something was better than nothing. Meanwhile, I've exceeded every sales quota with ease throughout my career, including in times of national economic woe and as recently as last year. What my most intractable sales reps failed to realize was that in offering me excuses to cushion their failure to get a better deal, they were actually advocating for the *customer!*

The only place for customer advocacy in a seller's game is in the creation of problem-solving deals that resonate with the customer's sense of self, how he carries himself personally and professionally, and where he wants to go. The Street-Smart seller's advocacy is never based solely on price, except as price is affected—*rises*—in step with our exploitation of the intangibles we gain by *listening*, by getting to the practical heart of what makes a customer tick.

In general, sales reps don't smell money, don't cultivate money; they chase money, uphill! They're just following scripts armed with technical knowledge that, incidentally, even incredibly, usually doesn't include an understanding of the idiosyncrasies of their own product line or those of the competition, a circumstance, incidentally, leaving a company wide open to complaints. Rarely does one of my customers call me to say a product isn't performing to expectations. Customers make calls like these to set up a future price cut, and they can be pretty sure they'll get it from other reps because price-cutting is the prevailing wisdom. But I'm 100 percent against it, and my customers know it. Price-cutting is a particularly dangerous game in the current sluggish economy, because ultimately it courts deflation. When prices get too low, they can get stuck there with dire consequences for all. Premium pricing is patriotic!

Not only do sales reps call me with their lackluster reports—of course, they e-mail me. And they e-mail clients. Frankly, they're crackberries. Almost nobody values the shelter of the spoken word anymore, or appreciates the vulnerabilities created by the existence of a cyber-paper trail—but this Street-Smart seller does because I came up during another time and I'm doing the advising. Believe me, the spoken word is a far more malleable thing than the written, and to the greatest extent possible sales business should be conducted in person or on the phone, *not* by e-mail. Claim that breathing space! Observe, experiment, and most of all, have some fun! Selling is just a challenging game. Really. And you can get rich playing high-stakes games if you just practice the skills I learned while being poor, the skills that allowed me to eat without stealing.

■　■　■

There is no way around the hard choices a person has to make to get out of the kind of poverty I experienced. I wish there were. When you come, as I did, from a poor family trying to scrape out an honest living, you learn that character and ability quickly reveal themselves in the face of adversity. Believe me, if you can survive poverty with no compromise to your honesty, you can make more money in sales than you ever dreamed of. Everything I learned about the honest hustle will distinguish me in sales because I know *people*. You can too, and if you follow my advice, you will.

Never forget how good it feels to be on the receiving end of assistance; that is the Street-Smart seller's secret weapon. Be a customer's problem-solver and champion, always making desired outcomes possible, and your call will always be welcome. Test my methods alongside your usual approaches and analyze the different results. You'll see that I'm right.

Above all, give yourself room to operate! Do your homework, be alert to unexpected openings and know where to look for them. In time, other sales reps will openly or secretly wish they had a little more of what you've got, your courage and flexibility. You won't be like everybody else in the best possible way. It will be a life-changing feeling, I can assure you. Remember: In the promised land of high premiums, the *Street-Smart* set the prices and everybody wins. To get started, visit www.streetsmartsalesman.com.

Notes

Introduction

1. Thomas J. Lueck, "Retail Center Is Proposed in East Harlem," *New York Times*, March 29, 1998.
2. Lisa Selin Davis, "A Landmark Struggle: In East Harlem, N.Y., Development Is Encroaching on Historic Property That Is Unprotected by Landmark Status," *Preservation Magazine* (online edition only), November 21, 2003.
3. Luciano J. Iorizzo and Salvatore Mondello, *The Italian-Americans* (New York: Twayne Publishers, 1971), 67, 108, 166, 169.

Chapter 2 The Million-Dollar Accident

1. Mark W. Johnston and Greg W. Marshall, *Sales Force Management* (New York: McGraw Hill/Irwin, 2006), 258–260.
2. Ibid., 261.

Chapter 4 Your Advantage Is That No One Takes You Seriously

1. Christine Galea, "2004 Compensation Survey," *Sales and Marketing Management*, May 2004: 28–34.
2. Mark W. Johnston and Greg W. Marshall, *Sales Force Management*, 8th ed. (New York: McGraw-Hill/Irwin, 2006), 38.

Chapter 5 Game-Changers

1. Roger Connors, Tom Smith, and Craig Hickman, *The Oz Principle: Getting Results Through Individual and Organizational Accountability* (Upper Saddle River, NJ: Prentice Hall Press, 1994).
2. Sam Dep, Lyle Sussman, and Sandler Systems, Inc., *Close The Deal: Smart Moves for Selling, 120 Checklists for Sales Success* (Cambridge, MA: Da Capo Press, 1999), xvii.
3. Anthony Holden, *Big Deal: Confessions of a Professional Poker Player* (New York: Penguin Books, 1990), 74.
4. David Mamet, *Writing in Restaurants* (New York: Penguin Books, 1986), 86.

Chapter 6 Shut Up!

1. Greg W. Marshall, Daniel J. Goebel, and William C. Moncrief, "Hiring for Success at the Buyer-Seller Interface," *Journal of Business Research 56* (2003): 247–255.

Chapter 8 Managing First Impressions

1. Steve Jeffes, *Appearance Is Everything* (Pittsburgh: Sterling House Publisher, 1998).

Chapter 9 A Sense of Urgency: Setting Priorities

1. Lionel Robbins, *An Essay on the Nature and Significance of Economic Science* (New York: New York University Press [1932], 1946), 16.

Chapter 16 Defy Expectations

1. William Keenan, Jr., "Who Has the Right Stuff?" *Sales & Marketing Management* (August 1993): 291–292.
2. R. Buckminster Fuller and E. J. Applewhite, *Synergetics: Explorations in the Geometry of Thinking* (New York: Scribner, 1975).

Chapter 20 Closing, or The Gentle Kill

1. David Mamet, *Writing in Restaurants* (New York: Penguin Books, 1986), 97.